FOUNDATIONS *of* LIFELONG LEARNING *and* PERSONAL TRANSFORMATION

Dr. Robert Wright and Dr. Judith Wright

Olga Tara
2822 Dundee rd., 14B
Northbrook, IL 60062
USA

Foundations of Lifelong Learning and Personal Transformation

EVOLATING
PRESS

ISBN 978-0-9849759-0-7

FOUNDATIONS *of* LIFELONG LEARNING *and* PERSONAL TRANSFORMATION

Dr. Robert Wright and Dr. Judith Wright

TABLE OF CONTENTS

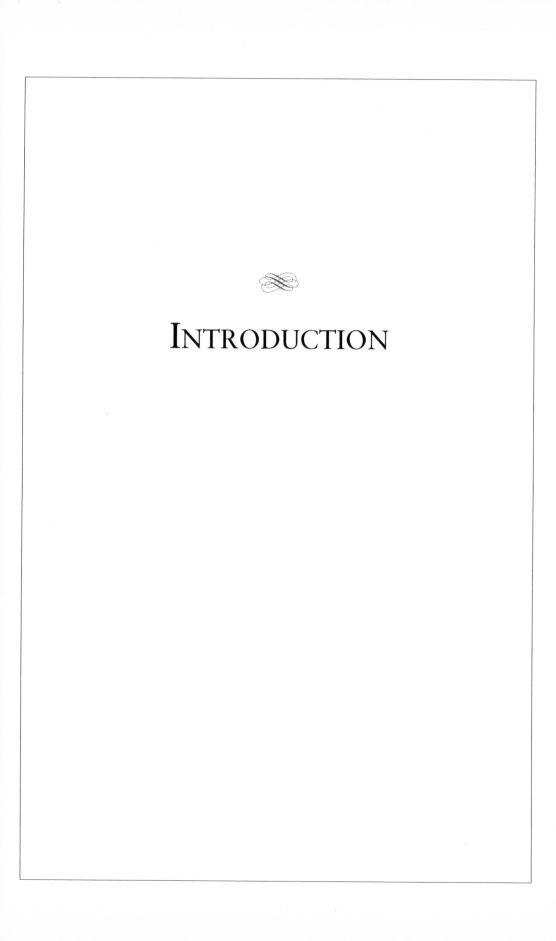

INTRODUCTION

INTRODUCTION

THIS BOOK PROVIDES YOU, THE LIFELONG LEARNER, with a solid, rich framework to facilitate your lifelong learning and personal development. It introduces you to a powerful system that you can use to make lasting, authentic changes, leading you to a more satisfying, fulfilling life. Just as a road map lets us go into places unknown, Foundations presents a map that allows you to journey courageously into the unknown of your potential self. It combines tried-and-true methodologies and philosophies into the Wright educational methodology, which takes the deepest human yearning for more in life through the psychological and philosophical underpinnings of human performance, to the theories and philosophies of high-performance learning and teaching, all based in current science and methodology.

The quest to realize your potential in all areas of life drives the educational experience at Wright, a lifelong education and learning organization dedicated to supporting your personal fulfillment and transformation. Our consumer and academic research over the past 35 years has led to the development of Wright Performative Education. Throughout this book, you will learn the academic and research foundations of Wright Performative Education and see how it is the logical synthesis and evolution of classic works in education, psychology, and philosophy going back millennia. Our state-of-the-art curriculum and learning technologies integrate for you the best of current neuroscience; Adlerian, developmental, humanistic, and positive psychology; existential philosophy; behavioral economics; educational theory and methodologies; and high performance research. At the same time, you will see how you can use those theories, methodologies, and technologies in your daily life to work toward and realize your full potential. Wright Performative Education features a multimodal delivery system of seminars and trainings, coaching, and laboratory learning that provides a map to help you realize your full potential, along with the guidance and assignments to make your quest an adventure of growth and discovery.

In this way, Wright Performative Education is part of the ongoing tradition of transformative learning described by Jack Mezirow and associates (2000). It involves a process of transforming your established ways of viewing yourself and others so that you can see yourself more clearly and, as a result, operate with a greater sense of purpose, personal efficacy, autonomy, and relatedness. In Mezirow's words:

> Transformative learning refers to the process by which we transform our taken-for-granted frames of reference (meaning perspectives, habits of mind, mind-sets) to make them more inclusive, discriminating, open, emotionally capable of change, and reflective so that they may generate beliefs and opinions that will prove more true or justified to guide action. . . Transformative Theory's focus is on how we learn to negotiate and act on our own purposes, values, feelings, and meanings rather than those we have uncritically assimilated from others—to gain greater control over our lives as socially responsible, clear-thinking decision makers (pp.7-8).

Indeed, students are typically drawn to Wright because they are searching for something more in their life—greater fulfillment, personal power, joy, love, service, and/or knowledge. Like them, you probably have reached a point where you are calling into question some of the basic beliefs and assumptions around which you have built you life and your personal identity. As a lifelong learner, you likely are continually engaged in a process of re-examination of those beliefs and assumptions. You probably have developed some degree of awareness of a gap that exists between the life you are currently living and the life you want to live— even if you cannot fully articulate all that this entails. You may want more career, relationship, or social success. You may recognize that there is a difference between the person you are presenting to the world and the more authentic person you yearn to be. The educational process at Wright is determined by your personal journey of self-knowledge and realization of potential. It leads you to increasingly authentic and powerful ways of being, knowing, and creative self expression.

A BRIEF HISTORY OF
WRIGHT EDUCATION

For over 40 years, the faculty at Wright have been studying, experimenting, and evaluating ways to help people reach their potential. Our formal research on human potential and effectiveness began in 1981, when Dr. Robert Wright began conducting consumer research in his business, Human Effectiveness Inc., which then consisted of a psychotherapy practice; a nationally-renowned managed care and employee assistance firm serving companies such as Neiman Marcus, BorgWarner, NutraSweet and many others; and a consulting and training practice. His research indicated that his clients were highly satisfied with the results they were getting from their individual coaching and group work. At the same time, however, they wanted to gain greater understanding of what they should be getting, how they should be getting it, what was good, what was enough, and how to get more.

Thus began a series of research projects leading to seminars specifically aimed at empowering clients—built around a powerful educational model that integrated Adlerian theory and group work with developmental and existential approaches to learning and personal growth. Dr. Wright's subsequent, iterative consumer research and seminars, with collaboration from Dr. Gordon Medlock and other colleagues, culminated in the Wright Model of Personal Growth and Development to which you will be introduced here. The Wright Model, presented in detail in Chapter 3, outlines a set of developmentally sequenced stages of consciousness that serve as a guide for lifelong learning and personal transformation. This model incorporates Alfred Adler's educational approach of identifying and confronting mistaken beliefs by experimenting with growth assignments that challenge these limiting beliefs while expanding the individual's behavioral repertoire of responses to life challenges. This gives students an experience of new ways of being, seeing, and acting. Further, the model encompasses the Adlerian notion that life can be viewed in terms of various spheres. As a student, you are called on to develop a vision for each sphere of life and learn the skills that would enable you to live a fulfilling and successful life in accordance with your ever-developing vision.

The Wright Model of Personal Growth and Development became the foundation of a series of experiential seminars and workshops designed to support individuals in the process of evolving toward higher levels of consciousness and personal functioning. The model includes a set of existential principles used to help students negotiate developmental tasks every moment and in every situation within the various spheres of life. The model and method focus on fulfilling deep emotional needs and concerns in the course of moving toward higher levels of consciousness and functioning. This model represents the first, and perhaps only, account of how existential principles can be used as the basis for a guided developmental process of lifelong transformational learning.

The notion of defined developmental stages leading to higher levels of consciousness and a sense of purpose is integral to the Wright curriculum. Lifelong learning and personal transformation are first and foremost a matter of growing awareness and expanded ways of being rather than outcomes. Outcomes and goal accomplishment happen at a high level because of changed thinking, feeling, and behaving. While each journey is unique to the individual, lifelong learning and personal transformation unfold according to predictable developmental stages. One of the unique features of the Wright model of transformational learning is that it incorporates the insights of Freud and psychoanalytic theory, which probed the sources of adult consciousness in unconsciously encoded early childhood experience. The Wright model pragmatically reframes the Freudian model within an Adlerian existential-developmental framework that focuses on addressing the full spectrum of human needs within the context of developing our full human potential.

In recent years, Dr. Robert Wright and Dr. Judith Wright have expanded upon their initial research as they observed something extraordinary taking place among certain students. Rather than making significant but incremental improvements in various areas of their lives, a select group of students were making quantum leaps. They were experiencing what psychologists refer to as second order change—sustained transformation that influenced everything in their lives from their relationships, to their careers, to their spirituality, regardless of their religion. They decided to investigate this phenomenon in a way they had never done before. They brought in a well-known researcher, Dr. Bill Seidman, whose area of expertise is "positive deviant research," identifying people who operate far above the mean. He interviewed Wright second-order change students over a three-day period. The Wrights and their staff then took those interviews and conducted further rigorous research.

Using the methodologies of grounded theory and action research in their doctoral work, the Wrights, for the first time, were able to identify and describe the moment-by-moment foundational process that provides the dynamic element to transformational perspectives, such as that of Ken Wilber and Clare Graves as presented by Beck and Cowan. They discovered the foundational framework for ongoing personal transformation that they call the process of Evolating, which consists of six phases for how individuals evolve toward the realization of elevating ideals. This discovery completed the current Wright educational methodology and conceptual framework for lifelong learning and personal transformation. The result is the more mature and evolved educational methodology of Wright Performative Education, which is the foundation of the Wright Graduate Institute and continues to serve students in seminars and trainings, learning laboratories, and coaching.

More details of Wright Performative Education are presented in Chapter 4. It creates an exciting and hitherto unseen level of educational synergy by drawing on revolutionary theories in performance training. It synthesizes coaching, classroom learning, and workshop training, by applying an assignment-based curriculum to specific areas of life including career, relationship, personal power, life purpose, and spirituality.

As a student, you are at the same time the researcher and the subject of your research. You are a lifelong learner and a theoretical investigator of the structures and processes that define, limit, and facilitate your personal transformation. You apply the methods of critical thinking, unbiased observation, and investigation to the study of personal power, family systems, group and organizational process, spiritual development, leadership theory and practice, coaching, and a wide variety of career areas that focus on the process of personal and social transformation. As both a participant and researcher, you consciously engage in the development of your own potential and transformation.

CHAPTER ONE

LIVING A GREAT LIFE

*Historical and
Theoretical Foundations
of Lifelong Learning*

CHAPTER ONE

LIVING A GREAT LIFE
Historical and Theoretical Foundations of Lifelong Learning

INTRODUCTION

IN THIS CHAPTER, DR. JUDITH WRIGHT lays the foundation for the philosophy and method that Wright uses to help lifelong learners maximize the quality of their life and learning. This chapter gives you a destination for your quest to realize your potential: an excellent life, a "great life," a life of More.

Wright has pioneered and developed a curriculum based on these traditions that not only awakens you to the possibilities of a life of More, but also provides you with both an innovative model that you can understand and practical skills that you can implement in your life.

The critical element is an essential choice you make, defined at Wright as the One Decision: a choice between more vs. More. It is a fundamental existential decision that underlines the importance of existential philosophy in the overall Wright philosophy, which will be discussed in Chapter 2, and it provides a way to give form and definition to the life you create.

This chapter emphasizes the benefits of orienting your life in congruence with your One Decision. This decision then guides you, the lifelong learner, in your choices in each moment, allowing you to reap the most from your days and achieve your dreams of fulfillment. Furthermore, using the One Decision, you can open more new opportunities for learning and growing than you had ever dreamed of previously, resulting in a life quest—the embodiment at Wright of a lifelong venture of learning, growing, and ongoing personal transformation which positively affects all areas of your life and the world around you.

The question of what makes a great life is universal and has been the subject of a long historical inquiry among philosophers, psychologists, and educators. In research done with Wright students and through extensive historical research, it is apparent that there is a universal longing for More in life—a concept that draws on multiple philosophical, spiritual, and psychological traditions. This longing, however, is often misinterpreted, with unintended and generally undesirable results.

Indeed, there is a difference between having more—more stuff, more achievement, more superficial desires—and the pursuit of the greater More in life—more meaning, satisfaction, engagement, and fulfillment. What does a great life consist of, and how is it fueled and motivated by the desire for More in life? As in many cases, the answer begins with the Greeks.

THE EXCELLENT LIFE

DEFINING THE IDEAL OF AN EXCELLENT LIFE has been a concern of mankind from the time of the first philosophers and spiritual leaders to present day psychologists, educators, and even economists. In the West, the ancient Greeks were the first to give a systematic account of what we mean by the good life. In the dialogues of Plato (Plato, 2003), Socrates defined the good life as a life that questions, a life of contemplation, the life of an inquiring and ever-expanding mind. Plato expounded on the good life as a harmoniously balanced life of fulfilling elements of reason, emotional drives, and, lastly, bodily appetites in proper order (Plato, 1941). Aristotle defined happiness as the pursuit of excellence and living virtuously (Aristotle, 1962). He claimed that what made us human was our rationality, and that human fulfillment came from living a balanced life of moderation, governed by rational choices. The philosophies of Plato and Aristotle have continued to be relevant throughout the ages, and are still referenced as guides to understanding what it means to live excellently.

Spiritual teachers and religious schools of thought have also addressed the question of how to live a good life. Gautama Buddha taught the Four Noble Truths. Jesus Christ taught "that all might have life and have it more abundantly" (John 10:10 New International Version). Hindu philosophers instruct followers to break the illusion of duality, which they term maya. Jewish and Judeo-Christian traditions teach the Ten Commandments as guides for right living. All religions, whether ancient or modern, address the question of how to live a good life.

Conversations on living a good life continued in the late nineteenth and early twentieth centuries through the expanding field of psychology as it began to focus on human behavior and mental processes. William James' Principles of Psychology (1890) provided a comprehensive account of psychological functions and processes. The work of Sigmund Freud defined the field of psychoanalysis and clinical psychology, with his focus on unconscious psychological processes and his recognition of the importance of early childhood experiences on adult development (Freud, 1953). The works of Alfred Adler and Carl Jung further developed the psychoanalytic perspective, with their focus on the mastery of social tasks (Adler, 1927) and individuation and spiritual development (Jung, 1939).

In the 1950s, humanistic psychology emerged with roots in existential thought, contemplating the essence, and emphasizing the importance of human experience. In the last several years, the relatively new field of positive psychology has sprung up to study the good life, well-being, and happiness. Martin Seligman, Albert Bandura, Mihaly Csikszentmihalyi, and many other empirical researchers are building upon the work and theories of such humanistic psychologists as Abraham Maslow, Carl Rogers, and Erich Fromm. Positive psychology research clusters into three overlapping areas: that is, the pleasant life defined as the life of enjoyment; the good life defined as the life of engagement; and the meaningful life defined as the life of affiliation (Seligman, 2002).

The field of education has also addressed aspects of training for the good life by embracing the concepts of vocational training, religious and spiritual education, preservation of cultural traditions and enculturation, career counseling, and development of life readiness skills. The American philosopher John Dewey defined the aim of education as the growth of the total human being, encompassing vocational and liberal education. He saw education as essential to full participation in democratic life, enhancing both the intellectual and social skills necessary for effective social participation (Dewey, 1938).

Although the concept of continual learning throughout life is not new, the field of "adult education" emerged in the twentieth century with an emphasis on lifelong learning. Its focus is enhanced living, far beyond preparation for a future job. Eduard Lindeman, an early pioneer in the field, saw that "education is life," and that "education conceived as a process coterminous with life revolves about non-vocational ideals...Its purpose is to put meaning into the whole of life" (Lindeman, 1926, pp. 4–5).

Another pioneer who articulated the idea of lifelong learning, Basil Yeaxlee, expressed this integrated vision of education as a part of living, which also echoes aspects of the ancient Greeks:

> But adult education, rightly interpreted, is as inseparable from normal living as food and physical exercise. Life, to be vivid, strong, and creative, demands constant reflection upon experience, so that action may be guided by wisdom, and service be the other aspect of self-expression, while work and leisure are blended in perfect exercise of body, mind and spirit, personality attaining completion in society. (Yeaxlee, 1929, p. 28)

THE DESIRE FOR MORE: THE MOTIVATION TOWARD AN EXCELLENT LIFE

Why all this focus on excellent living, the good life? Why has it been so important to mankind throughout history? Philosophers, scholars, psychologists, and spiritual leaders teach that the purpose of life is more than survival or procreation of the race. Within human beings is a desire, an urge, or even a calling or imperative to live life fully. As the philosopher Alan Watts stated, "Man is characterized by a hunger for the infinite, for an eternity of life, love and joy" (Watts, 1971, p.65). Carl Jung believed that our psyche has an innate urge for wholeness and self-realization (Jung, 1939). Robert L. Moore expanded upon the Jungian concept of the universal urge for wholeness and posited that everyone wants more out of life—whether it be more meaning, fulfillment, time, energy, status, respect, love, or spirit (Moore, 2002). Even rap artist Lloyd Banks, who named a recent album The Hunger for More, expands on this universal, yet individual, hunger for more:

> When I say The Hunger for More, it could be referring to more success. It could be more money. Or Respect. More power. More understanding. All those things lead up to that hunger for more, because my more isn't everybody else's more (Cohen, 2004).

The longing for More, inherent in each human being, is the call to the good life, to excellent living. This hunger, this appetite for more, is what compels man to pursue learning, growing, and contributing.

At Wright, the concept of the "longing for More" describes the fundamental motivation toward living an excellent life. The concept plays on a fundamental ambiguity in human existence, described primarily in the literature of existential philosophy, humanistic psychology, and contemporary interpretations of Buddhism. On the one hand, you have an urge for more pleasure, more things, more experiences, more joy, more money, more power, more prestige, more fame—more everything! Human beings have proven to have a virtually unlimited capacity to want more. On the other hand, human existence is characterized by a longing for a more meaningful existence, a spiritually fulfilling life, or both.

Existential Longing for More

In existential terms, the Danish philosopher Søren Kierkegaard described the underlying motivation of the spiritual life and our innate need for a meaningful existence as a longing for a relationship with the Infinite (Kierkegaard, 1938). The American theologian Paul Tillich described a focus on matters of ultimate concern—on matters of the ultimate meaning and purpose of life—as a fundamental motivation of spiritual life (Tillich, 1952). The atheist philosopher Friedrich Nietzsche referred to the will to power as fundamental to human motivation, by which he means a will to meaning and aesthetic creation (Nietzsche, 1967). The great twentieth century existential philosopher Martin Heidegger referred to man's connectedness with ultimate Being as the source of authentic existence, and the flight from Being as the cause of inauthentic forms of existence (Heidegger, 1962). At the core of these philosophies is a longing for a connection with the ultimate source of our being or existence as a fundamental motivation that transcends the sum of material wants we typically associate with the urge for more in everyday life.

Buddhist Longing for More

Buddhist philosophy introduces an important reinterpretation of this fundamental ambiguity in our longing for More. Buddhism proposes—one of the Buddha's four noble truths—that desire is the source of suffering. It is through material desire that we seek satisfaction and happiness and are ultimately disappointed. The disappointment arises because our deeper search is for a sense of permanence that will ensure an enduring happiness or fulfillment. All desire proves to be transitory, ultimately leaving us feeling empty and unfulfilled (Harvey, 1990).

Summarizing the Buddha's doctrine, Alan Watts explained that, "Man suffers because of his craving to possess and keep forever things that are essentially impermanent . . . This frustration of the desire to possess is the immediate cause of suffering" (Watts, 1960, p. 26).

Alternately, Buddhism postulates that the capacity for Nirvana or Bliss comes from the release from the cycles of desire and related suffering. By freeing ourselves from the cycle of desire, and through the meditative practices that open us to connection with the ultimate source of Being, we are opened to the possibility of Bliss through connection with this ultimate source. Zen Buddhism describes the ultimate source as nothingness. Hindu philosophy describes it as Atman or the World Soul. It is also described in various sects of Buddhism and Hinduism as transcendental consciousness—the source of all existence and meaning.

At first glance, this Buddhist interpretation of existence might appear to be inconsistent with the Wright concept of the Life of More. By saying that the goal of life is the cessation of desire, it would seem to be saying that a life of less—at least in terms of the pleasures of the body and material pleasure—is what is being advocated by Buddhism or Hinduism. Indeed, there is a strong ascetic tradition within Hinduism that advocates the denial of the pleasures of the body as the path toward spiritual enlightenment.

The Buddha, however, advocated a Middle Path between the extremes of asceticism and hedonism. His Middle Path required an important distinction that is often not clearly articulated in Buddhism: the distinction between desire without attachment and desire with attachment. It is ultimately the issue of attachment to the consequences or fruits of desire that leads to pain and suffering, according to the Buddha, not desire per se.

Western Psychology: Addictive Behavior vs. Healthy Desire

Western psychology has provided a way of interpreting this notion of desire with attachment that allows us to clarify what is central to the life of More. The crucial distinction can be described as that between addictive behavior and healthy desire. Addictions involve an attachment to a state of pleasure that becomes compulsive. It is described as a "high" or an altered state of consciousness, in which the addicted person experiences an intense rush of pleasure, which reinforces the behavior in question. The high can be like the high produced by cocaine, alcohol, or marijuana, which are called the hard addictions. The individual becomes so attached to the high that he or she cannot escape from the compulsion to repeat the addictive behavior. It becomes a trap from which the addict cannot usually escape without significant help.

This addictive behavior can also be observed in more subtle habits in which we develop an intense attachment to an altered state of pleasure. It could involve the attachment to the altered state or high one gets from shopping, exercising, watching television, or surfing the Internet. There are easily hundreds of such everyday behaviors where we develop an attachment to a desire that could be characterized as addictive. In the work of Dr. Judith Wright, based on her experience with Wright students and some of the things that have held them back in their growth, these forms of attachment are called "soft addictions" (Wright, 2003; Wright, 2006).

One might suggest at this point that almost any behavior could become a soft addiction. Aren't we always attached to pleasure, and don't we generally want to avoid pain? Don't we naturally tend to repeat pleasurable experiences and avoid painful ones? Aren't we overstating the case to call these addictions? And aren't we also overstating the case to say that these prevent us from reaching a state of higher consciousness or Bliss, such as is described through the meditative and other enlightenment experiences of Buddhism?

Dr. Judith Wright's pioneering work in the field of soft addictions, a term she coined in 1991, has revealed that soft addictions dramatically reduce the experience of life, leading to a life of less, not More. Engaging in soft addictions (the addictive use of activities, avoidances, ways of being, things) affects you in a number of ways: muting your consciousness, numbing your emotions, creating a sense of lethargy, and having a de-motivating effect. These habits are often accompanied by forgetfulness and an altered state described as being "out of it," buzzed, high, agitated, numb, lethargic, or non-responsive. Indulging in the mistaken "more" of soft addictions often results in a diminished ability to respond clearly or effectively (Wright, 2003, 2006). In fact, a recent study of multitasking with the Internet, email, the telephone, etc., revealed that it lowered an individual's IQ ten points (BBC News, 2005).

Experts in the field of addiction counseling have come to define addictive behavior as any mood-altering behavior that can adversely affect your relationships with others. This second feature, the adverse effect on relationships, provides you with the distinction needed to separate healthy from addictive desire. Our healthy desires in fact help us build satisfying relationships and honor our commitments to others and to ourselves. A desire such as thirst or hunger is naturally satisfied through a cool beverage or a nourishing meal. In this way the satisfaction of desire is a form of self-nurturing, which leads to a healthy and enhanced state of being. Healthy desires include the pleasure of meeting with a friend, engaging in your work, helping someone in need, completing a job that moves a project forward, and enjoying a concert or a game of tennis with friends. They do not include an element of avoidance, an attempt to escape from something, and they do not adversely affect your relationship with others. On the contrary, they help to support your well-being and nurture your relationships with others. Rather than diminishing your experience of life and leading to a life of less, meeting your true, deeper desires leads to the experience of a life of More.

Recent research in the relatively new field of positive psychology underlines this point. Your positive experience of life, your sense of happiness, does not occur through escape into addictive behaviors, but through deepening your engagement in life and by focusing on creating meaning. Studies on happiness reveal that it is not more stuff, indulging cravings, or more addictive behaviors that lead to happiness. Happiness is also not formulaic combinations of a good education, geography, marital status, income, etc. None of those intrinsically provide the good life. The research reveals that while happiness is related to experiencing pleasure (by savoring sensory experiences), it is engagement (depth of involvement with one's family, other people, and hobbies) and meaning (using personal strengths to serve some larger end) that are even more critical (Seligman, 2002). The research of existential psychologists Salvatore R. Maddi and Suzanne C. Kobasa also revealed that people with a sense of meaning, belonging, and direction are hardier, more resilient, and more satisfied (Maddi & Kobasa, 1984).

"This is newsworthy because so many Americans build their lives around pursuing pleasure. It turns out that engagement and meaning are much more important" (Seligman, 2002).

The Choice: Healthy Desire or Addictive Craving

This brings us finally to the question, or the decision, of whether to focus on healthy or addictive desire. This is the decision that ultimately decides the quality of your life, and specifically the choice to live a life of More. Yet, in the absence of a conscious choice to focus on fulfilling healthy desires, the default choice is to indulge in addictive cravings.

One of the key features of all desires, addictive or healthy, is that they include an element of what we at Wright call the spiritual longing for More. In the pursuit of any desire you seek some form of fulfillment, which can be viewed as a microcosm of your entire life. As will be discussed later in this chapter, this desire is embodied in the concept we call the "One Decision" to live a life of More, and the spiritual longing is embedded within the desire itself. The art of spiritual living, and the path to enlightenment and Bliss, is to be willing to make that choice to focus on the spiritual dimension of our material desire and to follow it toward its deeper and higher fulfillment.

Every act of desire can be described in spiritual terms as an effort to nurture oneself, to connect with one's embodied self, or to express love and connection with some aspect of reality—most often, another human being. This longing for connection with self and others is the everyday experience of spiritual longing that the philosophers and spiritual teachers described. It is available in every moment as a locus of control and focus for the direction of our life. At each moment, in each interaction, you are, in fact, confronted with the choice to pursue the spiritual dimension of your experience or to follow the addictive attachment to pleasure that ultimately takes you out of relationship with yourself and others, and with the ultimate source of your Being.

Throughout this book it will become more apparent how the various spiritual, philosophical, and psychological traditions have contributed to understanding the basic concept of the life of More. At Wright, we interpret these traditions and the ways in which spiritual practice can evolve from attending to your emotions, physical sensations, relationships, desires, and addictions—and from discerning the spiritual intent within your everyday experience. The educational practices through which this discernment can be cultivated and practiced in your life will be discussed in greater detail in Chapter 4.

THE EDUCATOR'S CHALLENGE

Although philosophers recognize the longing for More and psychologists indicate the importance of leading a satisfying life of More, we at Wright believe that it remains for the educator to assist people in learning how to live it. You don't typically interact with philosophers or psychologists as a matter of course in your development; you have and do, however, interface with education. The longing for More is an inherent human trait, and it is the educator's job to tap into this yearning for More—at every level, whether students are in preschool, graduate school, or involved in lifelong education. It is the lifelong educator's responsibility to help you reawaken the urge for More. Their task is to help you identify the deeper yearnings that will guide you to the More that is most fitting for you. Addressing the urge for More and kindling its flame help prepare you to become a lifelong learner, always seeking more in life.

The lifelong educator has a powerful responsibility—especially when you begin your quest for More—because for you, the learner, this urge may not have been fully understood and even misinterpreted, deadened, or misrepresented. Nietzsche posited that people often misrepresent themselves because they either do not understand where the urge for More comes from, or, in many cases, are ashamed of it (Wright, 2005). For the educator to influence you positively, she/he must help you access your genuine self and learn to develop from there. Further, the lifelong educator is in a unique position to expose you to the power of this yearning for More, to follow it to the good life, and to not mistake it or misinterpret it, wasting precious resources that take you off track from excellent living. Rollo May, a prominent existential psychologist, stated:

> I propose that the aim of education is...the widening and deepening of consciousness. To the extent that education can help the student develop sensitivity, depth of perception, and above all the capacity to perceive significant forms in what he is studying, it will be developing at the same time the student's capacity to deal with anxiety constructively (1967, p. 50).

In fact, the very term, "lifelong learning," implies that there is always something more to learn and that there is increased benefit to your life by continually reaching for more. Lifelong learning includes the process of discernment of life and spiritual direction, based on the concept of the One Decision, which is presented in depth in the next section.

THE WRIGHT PHILOSOPHY OF LIFELONG LEARNING

The Wright philosophy of lifelong learning and education stands on the shoulders of existentialists such as Sartre, Kierkegaard, and Nietzsche, and the other traditions mentioned above. The existentialists were far from the first to analyze the makings of an ideal life; scholars recognize the ancient Greeks as the first to document their investigation of self-improvement and ideal lifestyles. However, the Wright philosophy draws most fully from the existential philosophers. Additionally, the philosophy of More is grounded in the works of renowned psychologists like Sigmund Freud, Alfred Adler, and Viktor Frankl. Their writings and theories laid the foundation for the research, coaching, and training techniques developed at Wright, which in turn led to the development of the philosophy of More: living an excellent life.

The Wright philosophy is that there is a real, enduring More that you innately yearn for and that you have the ability to attain. This More—having a fulfilling life and having it abundantly in every moment—has eluded you because of the very human tendency to misunderstand what More actually is. People often haven't chosen to pursue the true More, and don't know how to effectively identify, achieve, and experience it. This section expands the experience of and thinking on what More is—and isn't, outlines the commitment needed to live it, and presents the context and skills you must develop to achieve and experience it.

WHAT IS—AND ISN'T—MORE

Students come to Wright because they want something more in their lives. For some it is a vague complaint or undefined sense of dissatisfaction, while for others it is a stated goal or problem they want to solve. Still others want to attain a magical solution—the one missing element that they believe will make them happy. Although the Wright curriculum and methodology honors this longing for More, part of the difficulty in our students attaining it is that they often don't know what More truly is and have confused this pure yearning for More with something quite less.

The yearning for More has inspired the highest of mankind's achievements and the most sublime of human experience (Wright, 2003). Yet this same urge for More is often misinterpreted as a craving for more material goods or superficial pursuits (Wright, 2006). From the images prevalent in current media through television shows, movies, books, magazines, advertising, etc., it appears that everyone wants more and even needs more in order to be happy. The good life seems to be defined by more material goods, money, and youth. If you believe advertising, the good life is achieved through a certain type of new car, designer suit, face cream, or bath product.

In this current climate of seeking and yearning, it seems that almost everyone has done something to try to get more in life—whether it is taking up art, doing yoga, losing weight, taking a class, getting a makeover, changing careers, buying lottery tickets, meditating, dropping out of the "rat race," getting married, buying bigger houses and fancier cars, or even getting rid of it all.

Indeed, the humanistic psychologist James Bugental (1967) suggested that this sense of lack and resulting search "comes not from being truly empty but rather emerges as a defense against the fear that we are powerless to change and direct our lives" (p.3). Yet even that statement reflects the desire to change and direct life while at the same time fearing that it isn't possible. You may well search to find the More you know exists, but may discover that you are often searching in the wrong places.

The attachment to your addictive desires, your own misinterpretation of these cravings as the More you seek, and the allure of quick-fix promises from media and advertisers all lead away from a life of More. Addictive cravings and soft addictions represent a mistaken attempt to experience More. Yet underneath each surface craving or compulsive wanting is a true desire for More.

In fact, the soft addiction itself can provide clues to your deeper longings. If you crave a bowl of ice cream, your deeper longing may actually be for comfort. If you compulsively want to share a juicy tidbit of gossip, it is likely that your deeper desire is for more contact, connection, belonging, or a sense of feeling important. Your attachment to television could represent a deeper desire to be connected or stimulated, while the compulsive checking of email could signal the desire to connect, to belong, or to matter (Wright, 2003; Wright, 2006). As you learn to recognize the purity and importance of these deeper desires and the longing for More, you can begin to learn the skills to consciously pursue the fulfillment of the true desire for More.

More isn't satisfying every craving, and it does not mean that you are in a perpetual state of Bliss. More does not mean a single transcendent moment, or complete happiness at all times. The real More is not even an action or a step, but a shift in perspective that completely transforms the fabric of your life (Wolfert, 2003). As the existentialists and positive psychologists have suggested, More means viewing life as an adventure, living every moment, and engaging in what is in front of us as fully as possible. More means designing a life where these rich moments are the norm of our experience, not the exception.

Some people think a life of More is financial wealth. Others believe it involves sitting on a mountaintop meditating eight hours a day, or repeating affirmations, or divesting themselves of wealth, or quitting their job to pursue a life of service. Some discover that More is not in these things and, in fact, there is no formula at all. Although a life of More may include all of these, they are by-products, not an end in themselves. A life of More is a shift in perspective from attachment-focused desire and addictive behavior to healthy desire, emotional fulfillment, and spiritual fulfillment. In fact, as lifelong learners begin to pursue More in life directly, they often find that soft addictions seem to loosen their grip and become much less interesting when compared to the fulfillment of the deeper desires.

The Wright philosophy suggests that More is available for anyone who wants to discover what it takes to experience life abundantly and is willing to do the work it requires. As existentialist philosophers contend, all people have the ability to make choices that shape their lives and, from a deeper perspective, create their essence. Many people attempt to become what we at Wright call lifelong learners; they desire to expand their knowledge, wisdom, and abilities through personal growth throughout their entire lives. However, in their search for ways to improve themselves and increase their daily fulfillment, these people often come to dead-ends, and their attempts do not deliver the results for which they had hoped.

First of all, they tend to aim at short-term solutions, and short-term fulfillment and satisfaction tend not to last. Likewise, they worry that the small moments of insight that they experience do not add up to something suitably big, and they keep searching for a greater meaning. They lead partially successful or "better" lives, but things are always falling through the cracks; they achieve at work but face failing relationships; they have a great family life but poor health; or they achieve good health but experience career problems. At certain moments, they even touch the greater More that we all yearn for—the sense of rightness with the world, the feeling of being part of something larger, a sense of well being despite fear or challenges, a flash of insight in a difficult situation, a cathartic release after crying, or the excitement of approaching life as an adventure. These moments of insight push the lifelong learner to keep seeking the More they know exists, but that they do not yet possess in daily abundance.

THE COMMITMENT TO A LIFE OF MORE: THE ONE DECISION

According to the Wright philosophy of More, there is one existential decision, a choice that makes all the difference if a person is to live a life of More. This fundamental life choice is what Dr. Judith Wright calls the One Decision. Once made, that decision becomes a fundamental commitment to that individual's quality of life that serves as a touchstone for all other moment-to-moment life choices. Having made this One Decision, it becomes a benchmark for all other decisions. The One Decision is a contextual choice to live life according to a deeper commitment, a dedication to pursue an excellent life, a life of More. As Jung suggests, "Trust that which gives you meaning and accept it as your guide" (Mialaret, 1976, p. 91) The One Decision is a binary choice: the choice to live an excellent life and to follow the longing for more satisfaction and fulfillment in life, as opposed to pursuing addictive cravings. With this One Decision, it is easier to differentiate the choices that are in alignment with it, such as choosing aliveness versus dead-ness, engagement versus detachment, being genuine versus inauthentic, telling the truth versus lying, and so forth.

A One Decision is a commitment to how you will lead your life, focusing on the quality of life. While your life purpose speaks to why you live, and your goals deal with what you do, the One Decision addresses how you live your life. Examples of One Decisions are:

> *I am a stand for truth.*
> *I am awake, alive, and engaged.*
> *I live my life as if every moment matters.*
> *I am a vessel for spirit.*
> *I am a woman of integrity.*
> *I follow my deepest desires.*
> *I live with an open heart.*

Using the concept of the One Decision, you begin consciously determining the quality of your life rather than just letting life happen. Self-determination and engagement in creating the quality of your own life become a series of conscious choices, moving toward self-fulfillment and self-knowledge. In the absence of a conscious One Decision, there is a default decision based on mistaken beliefs, which leads to following cravings as substitutes for true desire. These mistaken beliefs pull you strongly away from a life of More and into a state of fear and mis-interpretation of the world.

Making and living a One Decision brings about transformational shifts in your life, not just incremental growth. When you live according to your One Decision, you may transcend step-by-step personal learning and growth; its oper-ation actually transforms your life. Rather than adding spiritual or enriching activities to your life, like condiments to a meal, these activities flow from your deeper yearnings and start to become the main course.

The philosophy of the One Decision to live a life of More is also rooted in Kierkegaard's notion that life hinges on a single basic choice to be a self, or to flee from self-hood into a world of pleasure, addiction, and escape from responsibility and commitment. His famous quote, "Purity of heart is to will one thing" (from the meditative book of the same title) parallels what Dr. Judith Wright termed the One Decision (Kierkegaard, 1938). The one decision for Kierkegaard—the fun-damental Either/Or of life—is to choose to live as an ethical/spiritual being. This means ethical in the sense of living a life based on commitment to principle, as evidenced in the choice of marriage. To be spiritual is to open yourself to the fundamental ground of your being—the relationship to the transcendent or God, which is the very basis of your selfhood. To be a self, as Kierkegaard so eloquently and somewhat mysteriously described, "is to relate oneself to oneself through relating oneself to another" (Kierkegaard, trans. 1992). The primary relationship for Kierkegaard is the relationship to the Infinite or God as mediated through the life and example of Christ. Taking it a step further, which Kierkegaard also does in his writings on love, you can say that it is through your relationship with all others, as expressed in brotherly love, that you come to a full experience of your own self-hood (Kierkegaard, 1962, 1992).

A LIFE OF MORE: THE LIFE PROJECT

Core to the One Decision is the concept of shaping your life through your choices, a theme of the existential philosophers and psychologists. This focus becomes what French existentialist Jean-Paul Sartre deemed a "life project"—what we call at Wright the "life quest."

Sartre saw each human life as a project, self-defined and powerful. Each person is "what he wills, and as he conceives himself after already existing… Man is nothing else but that which he makes of himself" (Sartre, trans. 1978, p. 4). For the existentialists, a person's existence precedes his essence. This is a crucial principle because it runs counter to the main thrust of Western thought from Plato to Hegel, via Judaism, Christianity, and Descartes. What it claims is that there is no a priori conception of humankind, whether as a species or as individuals. Sartre presented the notions of human agency or choice, and the notion of the life project (Medlock, 1986).

The Wright philosophy of a life quest, a life focused on the choice to live the life of More, relates to Sartre's concept of the life project. This life quest includes the One Decision, vision, and the tools you need to support living a One Decision. Wright embraces Sartre's existential belief in self-determination through choice. Additionally, we agree that this self-formative freedom cannot be escaped, even in its difficult or oppressive moments.

Kierkegaard argues that life is suffering—unless you consciously choose to live it as a progressive adventure. To Kierkegaard, your life project is ideally one of a progression from a life of pleasure, to a life of commitment, to a life of faith or spirituality. If you see life as something to endure, to suffer, to manage, or to keep familiar, you experience less. You embrace the true More only when you choose to view life as a risky venture in which you leave your comfort zone and bet on aliveness (Kierkegaard, 1959, p. 22).

To succeed as a lifelong learner, you stretch, discover, and achieve your heart's desire, but you first must recognize that you have the ability to shape yourself and your future. In the adventure of living as a lifelong learner, you come to understand yourself, your true self, in order to sense your deep urges and use them to form your vision. The existentialist philosopher Friedrich Nietzsche emphasized the importance of finding authenticity, living by truthfulness, and exposing hypocrisy. Indeed, he believed that the pursuit of truth was linked to the experience of aliveness. He criticized the morality of the priests, as he described it, for advocating repression of the body and for advocating a notion of morality and God that was used to deny the most powerful and exuberant aspects of the human personality. Nietzsche opposed the ascetic path of religion and advocated a new path that celebrated the expression of vitality and aesthetic creation (Nietzsche, 1967).

Focusing great amounts of attention on recovering aliveness and vitality, Nietzsche attempted to identify and dismiss the hypocrisy of Victorian morality. For him, the truth was inextricably tied with the dismissal of religion and of the existence of God, though this is not a belief we hold at Wright. At the same time, however, the Wright philosophy does reflect Nietzsche's focus on seeking truth about your situation and yourself in order to live honestly and with integrity.

INFLUENCES OF FREUDIAN AND ADLERIAN PSYCHOLOGY

Regarding psychology's influence on the Wright philosophy, Sigmund Freud's original concept of looking inside to understand yourself plays a key role. Therefore, his philosophy holds a great deal of influence on teaching methods at Wright. Freud's development of psychoanalysis and his study of the unconscious brought into being a new way to examine human behavior (Freud, 1953). Though Western scholars have since dismissed many of Freud's teachings, such as his focus on sexuality, his fundamental precepts remain influential and are present in the Wright philosophy and methodology.

Alfred Adler expanded upon Freud's theories, proposing that what people believe becomes their experience, not because they lack options but because they choose to behave in ways that support their existing beliefs about the world. The existentialist school of thought shares Adler's focus on self-determination, as does Wright. During his practice as a physician, Adler stressed the importance of seeing patients in relation to their total environment, and he began developing a humanistic, holistic approach to human problems. Moreover, Adler developed a flexible, supportive psychotherapy to direct his patients toward maturity, common sense, and social usefulness (Adler, 1997). The Wright philosophy strongly aligns with Adler and the existentialists' emphasis on the power of choice, the importance of a humanistic approach, and a flexible and supportive process toward self-improvement.

LIFE QUEST

The Wright philosophy of living a great life recognizes the longing for More, the importance of committing to pursuing a great life, and the need for engaging in what Sartre termed your life project, further defined at Wright as a life quest. Your life quest includes developing a vision of More in life and engaging in the quest for the fulfillment of that vision. The life quest includes a process of discernment of spiritual intention in everyday life, to free you from a life of attachment to addictive behavior in all its various forms.

In order to live a life of More, you as a lifelong learner must grasp the importance of the One Decision and then consider the importance of this decision in the journey ahead. This decision then guides your life quest (Wright, 2005). Indeed, the One Decision makes the difference between doing spiritual things and living a spiritual life, between doing good things and living a good life.

Like many lifelong learners, you may begin this journey by first thinking you have to travel far, but you will soon discover that the journey is one of going more deeply and fully into the challenges facing you already, every day, in every moment. This does not mean that your vision or your One Decision is small. A life quest requires visioning things that matter, yearnings from your open heart that inspire you to quest after what best-selling author Jim Collins calls BHAGs: big hairy audacious goals (Collins, 2001, p. 89).

With your One Decision guiding you, you as a lifelong learner will grow to quest after things that really matter to you—love, spirit, making a difference, or even making more money or building a successful business—compelling you to do something you would not do otherwise, such as taking risks while reaching for something higher. The point is not which of your desires you may choose to follow, but rather your capacity to discover the personal intent within your desire and to develop that aspect of your experience as your life project. Working this philosophy, Wright guides lifelong learners to create a vision for their lives and to create quests both great and small (Wright, 1992).

Lifelong learners then discover that the adventure has been there all along, and that it is simply a shift in perspective that allows you to see life as an odyssey. You will see and embrace previously unrecognized challenges, difficulties, rewards, celebrations, and excitement as you learn to pursue a life of More. This journey has led Wright students to create meaningful relationships, to positively transform work environments, and to affect national policy on issues that matter to them. Students have not only transformed their own lives, but have also had a positive impact on their families, their communities, and their world.

CHAPTER TWO

LIFELONG LEARNING

*The Educational, Philosophical, and
Psychological Foundations*

CHAPTER TWO

LIFELONG LEARNING
The Educational, Philosophical, and Psychological Foundations

INTRODUCTION

AS A LIFELONG LEARNER INTERESTED IN DEVELOPING *to your fullest potential in all areas of life, you can gain perspective on your life and its growth trajectory by studying various schools of philosophy and psychology. These schools look at the human being from different perspectives, allowing you to glean lessons from different viewpoints on how people develop, learn, and grow. In this chapter, Dr. Robert Wright orients you to the educational, psychological, and philosophical foundations of the Wright philosophy of living a great life, introduced in Chapter 1. This gives you a view of the overall geography of lifelong learning, the terrain of your journey toward the realization of your potential.*

After decades of working with individuals and delivering trainings to lifelong learners, Dr. Wright has found that three schools of philosophy and psychology have proven particularly useful in helping learners develop, attain success, and experience fulfillment in all areas of life: 1) Adlerian psychology, 2) developmental psychology, and 3) existential philosophy. As this chapter shows, these fields provide a rich foundation for the practical educational methodologies and technologies used at Wright.

This chapter presents the consumer research Dr. Robert Wright and colleagues conducted to enhance client satisfaction and growth. This research became the foundation of Wright's integrative approach to lifelong learning and led to the incorporation of Adlerian, developmental, and existential approaches, which are explained in the remainder of this chapter. You will see how Wright operationalizes those fields into practices that enhance the daily lives of lifelong learners and how the Wright philosophy has evolved from client experience and practice.

A CONSUMER RESEARCH
FOUNDATION

As a way of enhancing service to their clients in the early 1980s at Human Effectiveness Incorporated, Dr. Robert Wright and his colleagues developed and delivered consumer satisfaction surveys to individuals and groups. In reviewing results, it was apparent that students all agreed on the value of the training they were receiving but at the same time they wanted to gain greater understanding of what they should be getting, how they were getting it, what was good, and what "enough" was.

Dr. Wright and his colleagues examined the training they were delivering as well as their own psychological training and orientation. They realized that at the time they generally oriented to the existential school of learning and development. From the perspective of a lifelong learner, however, that seemed too complicated and abstract.

They also felt a significant debt to Sigmund Freud, Alfred Adler, and Carl Jung. From an educational point of view it was Adler's approach to seeing people in their social world that they found most compelling. Additionally, they felt that Adlerian psychology made the existential philosophy operational. Adler's idea that humans were striving and driving toward perfection and an ideal was a direct crossover to the existential idea of a life project and its Wright corollary, the life quest, as introduced by Dr. Judith Wright in Chapter 1.

Dr. Robert Wright chose to use the Adlerian "spheres of existence," which he called "areas of life," as a focal point around which to apply the existential concept of vision. Dr. Wright and his colleagues expanded Adler's original spheres into seven areas of life and had students identify their vision in each area. Each student's vision for him or herself in each of the seven areas of life became a map for learning and growth. At specific intervals, students reviewed their growth and development against the visions they had created.

Students felt this was useful, but they still wanted more. They wanted to understand the methodologies and mechanics of psychological training and growth in order to develop faster and mark their growth and progress more effectively. They felt that there was still something that the training staff was not telling them.

In an effort to provide students more grounding in the psychological and philosophical foundations of the work in which they were engaged, Dr. Wright and his colleagues re-examined the work they were doing and the trainings they were delivering and realized that although they did not agree with the Freudian concept of pathology, they did use a teleological developmental framework; they saw humans as developing purposefully toward an end point, just as Freud did. They also realized that much of the work that they were doing had a developmental basis.

In examining developmental perspectives, they ruled out Freud because his work was so deeply steeped in a pathological orientation. Dr. Wright felt that Erikson's concept of choice was useful and related to existential perspectives but decided that his phases were too limited. For example, Erikson's stage of autonomy versus shame (toddlerhood) missed the importance of issues of affirmation and emotional hunger that Dr. Wright found to be critically important (Erikson, 1993). Kohlberg's (1984) theory of moral development was also too limited, in that it was too focused on the cognitive aspects of development and ignored the emotional or relational aspects. Maslow's (1968) theory was also too limited, emphasizing a hierarchy of needs that was not really developmental. He provided a notion of a hierarchy of needs, but not an analysis of developmental stages throughout the life cycle or a model of growth from one stage to the next.

As a result, Dr. Wright and his colleagues began developing their own model from these and others. They examined the developmental model of G. M. Durst and found it lacking in positive vision (Durst, 1982). They found the holodynamic model of Vern Woolf to be interesting but too metaphysical and lacking in depth in human development; they did borrow Woolf's bimodal dynamic and adapted it to their model, which will be seen later (Woolf, 1990).

Students embraced this but still asserted that they did not have all the information they needed to provide a useful framework for their lifelong learning. At this point, Dr. Wright and his colleagues decided to integrate the existential approach, for the first time developing an integrated Adlerian / developmental / existential framework.

ADLERIAN PSYCHOLOGY

Alfred Adler was an Austrian psychiatrist practicing in Europe in the early 20th century. He became famous for coining the term "inferiority complex" and for developing individual psychology. A key student of Freud, he focused, however, on humans as social beings, constantly learning and growing. Adlerian psychology is a very practical and accessible approach to learning and development, providing an excellent foundation for personal growth. Adler saw education as a primary mission of his, and to Dr. Robert Wright, Adler is the most didactic of the traditional theorists in psychology. He studied Adler's theoretical approach most extensively, and it was the first approach used in developing Wright's integrative educational model of personal growth and development. In that context especially, the Adlerian perspective has helped guide Wright students in problem solving and growth plans and can do the same for you.

Adler believed that you create your experience through your beliefs, both accurate and inaccurate. According to Adler, beliefs are unconsciously held and determine the choices you make in life. Your beliefs represent your attitudes about what you can expect from the world, what the world expects of you, and what is allowed and not allowed. Adler felt that adults could shift their unconsciously directed behavioral patterns and programming by uncovering what we call mistaken beliefs and learning new behaviors that are contrary to those indicated by those beliefs (Adler 1927).

Adler believed that your earliest life experiences are the foundations of your mistaken beliefs. For example, if you have been severely undernourished in early life, it will affect your conclusions about the nature of the world—what it expects of you and what you can expect of it. From this early experience of undernourishment, you conclude that the world does not have what you need, that it takes a lot from you while giving little in return, and that you must suffer for whatever you get, no matter how little it is. This constellation of mistaken beliefs then determines your behaviors in life, and you act in ways to keep your world in line with those beliefs.

According to Adler, you create your life as a projection of those limiting beliefs in a self-fulfilling prophecy. In other words, what you believe becomes your experience, not because it is the only option, but because you choose to operate in ways that affirm your beliefs about the nature of reality. For example, a person who believes that the world returns little for significant investment will unconsciously ask for and expect little, thereby affirming that the world conforms to this unconsciously held belief.

Rudolph Dreikurs, a prominent student of Adler who brought Adlerian theory to the United States, put the complex of beliefs into a concept he referred to as "the lifestyle." The lifestyle is a summary of your beliefs and ways of behaving. As a student and lifelong learner, you can learn to shift the limiting elements of your lifestyle and maximize your potential by identifying basic mistakes and self-defeating apperceptions, or limiting beliefs. By challenging these elements, you can operate in new ways and implement new behaviors that your old beliefs would have prohibited (Beames, 1984), thereby challenging limiting beliefs and breaking out of the self-fulfilling prophecy cycle described above.

For example, if you think anger is harmful, you have likely repressed your anger consciously and unconsciously. You probably have not learned to use anger appropriately and effectively, because you believe that the world will not tolerate your anger and that you are wrong for even feeling it. You can, however, learn to recognize these limiting beliefs and behaviors and challenge them by experimenting with new behaviors. In this case, experiments in the expression of anger can be used to test your newly recognized unconscious assumptions. Through exercises and assignments that build your skills, you will be able to express your dislikes, disagree with others, and even criticize and pick fights. You will discover that it is not always harmful to express anger, and, in fact, that it can be beneficial. You will likely develop new beliefs and distinctions, be able to discriminate between different types of anger, and also be able to identify expressions that are more or less effective as well as more or less to your liking.

Each time you engage in a behavior, such as expressing anger that would have been prohibited by a limiting belief, you expand your repertoire and, as a result, your ability to be effective in the world. In challenging and changing beliefs you can improve your overall way of being and lifestyle and continue to maximize your abilities (Schulman & Dreikurs, 1978). In this process, you can change the dynamics of your self-fulfilling prophecy and develop new ways of living outside old belief systems and subsequent limitations.

In addition to his insights about limiting beliefs, Adler divided life into areas or spheres. He initially identified three key life areas: intimacy/family, work, and social (community/friendship). The social area of community and friendship represented an extension beyond Freud's framework that had emphasized love (intimacy) and work as the two key areas of focus for personal learning. Adler's focus on the social aspect of being and the development of social feeling (Gemeinschaftsgefühl) as the defining mark of good mental health led him to emphasize the social domain of life as a key area for learning and growth. Later, Adlerian theorists added self and spirituality to the list of key life areas. Self included the domain of beliefs, feelings, and self-concept while spirituality included the realization of higher ideals and values.

As described in the Introduction, the 1981 consumer survey of students at Human Effectiveness Incorporated revealed that they felt thankful for the power of the services they were receiving—such as coaching, counseling, and growth groups. They did not, however, appreciate the fact that they felt ignorant about the overall context of their growth—what they should be getting, what constituted excellent versus poor progress, and what was enough. In response to this feedback, Dr. Robert Wright began developing a course at Wright that is now called Vision in Action.

The Vision in Action course allows students to develop a practical vision for their life, as well as immediate goals, in each area of life. By focusing on the distinct issues and goals within each area, students begin to significantly enhance their growth and development. The vision guides their growth and development, and they revisit it in trimester progress reviews. In working with students to develop the course, Dr. Wright and his colleague, Dr. Gordon Medlock, expanded Alfred Adler's original spheres of life, intimacy/family, social, and work (Adler, 1927/1962), into seven areas of life along a relationship axis as follows: relationship to body, self, family, others, work, principles and society, life purpose, and higher power. This model incorporated the areas of self and spirituality and also went beyond the other models in describing a continuum of consciousness from body to life purpose and higher power.

As a lifelong learner, you should find it extremely powerful to direct your attentions and efforts toward visions of possibility in each of these seven areas. By focusing your attention on a higher vision, you can enhance your development by establishing clearer goals, picking assignments or experiments to accomplish these goals, and regularly reviewing and modifying your goals. By combining a powerful vision for your life with a human development perspective, you are well on your way to maximizing your potential for joy, satisfaction, service, and development. To see how vision works, however, it is important to understand the perspective of developmental psychology and its role in the Wright philosophical and educational model.

DEVELOPMENTAL PSYCHOLOGY

Psychologists have been studying human development and the refinement of our highest capacities for well over 2,000 years. In ancient Greece the ideal human developed excellences or virtues in the areas of mind, body, and spirit, including both personal and political life. Today, in current psychology, developmental models abound. They generally analyze human development through the life cycle. Often, they are teleological and recognize an ideal, complete, or full human development. They also frequently identify ways individuals can become stuck or fixated, failing to develop fully. As a lifelong learner, these models give you ideals toward which you can aim your development. They also give you methods of analysis to understand ways you become stuck in your development and consequently, your life. You gain insight to deal with the problems you encounter. You often move beyond stuck points and thereby develop further, adding to the richness and effectiveness of your life.

These models of human growth and development generally occupy themselves with your development throughout your life. Some developmental approaches track your development in consciousness, while others track moral development, ego maturation, and the evolution of your needs. They have been formulated by well-known psychologists discussed earlier, including Freud, Erikson, Piaget, Kegan, Kohlberg, and Maslow, as well as by the lesser known practitioners and theoreticians, Wolf, Loevinger, Ichaso, Graves, and many more.

Perhaps developmental theories are so common because they identify what Gail Sheehy (1976) described as the "predictable crises of adult life," and as a result, they give you key tools in understanding and mastering yourself. They can be invaluable to you because they provide virtual maps for getting the most out of your life—particularly during periods of transition and change. They give you a way to think about, assess, and identify your needs. Additionally, they often provide an ideal or vision toward which you can develop.

In developing the Wright philosophy, the models mentioned above were insufficient for the positive development that Dr. Wright wished to enhance in his approach to learning. For example, Kohlberg's model of moral development was too limited, Erikson's model was not easily applied in daily life, and the Freudian or ego psychology models were too pathological and limited to empower development of human potential as we envisioned it. Third Force psychologist Abraham Maslow provided a strong model, but it lacked internal dynamic elements to make it applicable in daily life. Dr. Wright and his colleagues decided to leverage the insights from the various developmental models, but placed them within an existential-humanistic context as stages in the development of consciousness. They followed Erik Erikson's initial framework because it identified each stage as involving a fundamental choice between two polarities. His eight stages and the choices at each stage were the following:

1. Trust / Distrust
2. Autonomy / Shame & Doubt
3. Initiative / Guilt
4. Industry / Inferiority
5. Identity / Role Confusion
6. Intimacy / Isolation
7. Generativity / Stagnation
8. Integrity / Despair

The sense of choice at each stage seemed particularly important to human development as a process of progressive stages of consciousness. It implies that you have a choice about your existence at each stage, with the focus of personal learning on helping to choose the healthier option at each level.

Dr. Wright and his colleagues disagreed, however, with some of Erikson's findings, such as when he says that the fundamental issue of toddlerhood is that of Autonomy vs. Shame and Doubt. They saw the fundamental issue as one of the development of a sense of self, with the implication that a hunger for affirmation defined this phase. They saw the primary question or challenge here as a choice between hunger and affirmation; the need to be recognized and affirmed appeared to be more fundamental than the struggle for autonomy, which they did incorporate into their next phase, reactivity vs. assertion. Based on the evidence of work with clients and students, Dr. Wright saw that a person's need to be affirmed both in their capacity for autonomy and in the depth of their feelings and hungers, was the fundamental issue facing toddlers—and also adults who are dealing with those issues later in life. These differences led to a very different model, which is the subject of Chapter 3.[1]

The non-pathological model of G. Michael Durst did not point to sufficient positive states, and the bi-modal model of Verne Woolf missed important stages and was too metaphysical in nature for direct application to daily life.

Freud and ego psychologists used clinical language for stages of development: the oral, anal, phallic, latency, and genital stages. These models focused exclusively on early childhood and were primarily concerned with psychopathology. In these respects they differed from Erikson, who focused on the entire life cycle and had a more teleological focus toward healthy development.

Kohlberg's framework for moral development provided another useful perspective. As he describes moral development, at the earliest stage of development children strive to maximize pleasure and avoid punishment. During the next stage, which is characterized by conformity to social rules, the child demonstrates respect for and duty to authority. The child also seeks to avoid disapproval from that authority. As the child matures, his or her moral judgment is motivated by respect for legally determined rules and an understanding that these rules exist to benefit all. Eventually, universal principles are internalized. These principles, such as liberty and justice, may even transcend aspects of the existing legal system (Kohlberg, 1984).

---

[1] Note: The Wright developmental framework is similar in many respects to the development theories of Ken Wilber. Dr. Robert Wright did not read Wilber's work at the time they were developing their framework, but in retrospect it is clear that both are attempting to integrate existential and Eastern models of development with the traditional Western psychoanalytic developmental models (Wilber, 1980).

It was not until many years later that we were introduced to the work of Dr. Clare W. Graves. Dr. Graves traces the development of human social systems from individual survival to tribal, social, and more complex societies (2002).[2] At Wright, we believe that Dr. Graves' model brilliantly demonstrates the familiar phrase, "ontogeny recapitulates phylogeny." In analyzing the evolution of human society, he shows how individual development follows the same analogous path. He shows how some societies or systems, as he discussed them, are not fully developed, just as individuals are limited in development. He also shows differences and variations in thought, value, communication, and interaction at the different levels.

Graves outlines his developmental levels beginning with individual survival. Tribal affiliation follows with the emergence of mighty societies such as Greece and Rome, roughly, in his third level of development. These complex societies focused on domination and expansion. Developmentally, these societies followed Graves' second level, the tribal systems, which themselves followed the most basic level, individual survival. After these large, powerful societies, where might makes right, Graves takes us developmentally to the monastic or saintly systems (level four), first seen in the West during the Dark Ages.

Level five systems for Graves are focused on mastery of the world or physical universe. They tend to be industrial and commercial in nature. Mastery of the physical universe in our world was marked by the Industrial Revolution—only to lead to times of social concern such as socialism, communism, and the rise of the welfare state, Graves' level six. In the future, not yet realized, Graves sees a level seven: cognitive, ideal, principle-driven living that would ultimately lead to a possible level eight: connected, unified, harmonious, concerted living in which the individual, environmental, and societal needs are finally reconciled in a fully conscious, spiritually enlightened scenario.

As you will see more clearly in Chapter 3, the Graves model and the Wright Model of Personal Growth and Development have significant similarities. For you, the lifelong learner, Graves demonstrates how you evolve from totally dependent, fighting to stay alive (Graves' as well as our level one) to belonging and developing an identity, Graves' level two, tribal (Morningstar, 1981) and our level two, hunger and affirmation. You become aware of power and want to master your world at level three, marked typically by the "terrible twos," as well as Graves' level three, marked by societies seeking to dominate other societies. This is fol-

---

[2] See the Appendix for a compilation and comparison of developmental approaches by Dr. William Lee, a dutiful archivist of Dr. Graves' work.

lowed by another period of conformity where belonging to the peer group in adolescence is of utmost importance, level four. You then begin to address mastery of
your world as a young adult in level five of our model, as well as level five of
Graves', and develop greater concern for deeper meaning and a perspective on the
whole in level six. Our model sees striving at level five followed by the development of a sense of purpose and responsibility at level six.

Not all of you, developmentally, make it to a point where you are living most
of your life in a state of emotional adulthood, levels five and above. As you will
see later, theoreticians and researchers from Loevinger to Maslow find that fewer
than 20% of the population and as few as 5% develop emotionally, psychologically, and morally beyond adolescence, level four of Graves', as well as level four
of the Wright model, and of Durst's (Durst, 1982).

Abraham Maslow was a developmental theorist who is one of the founders
of humanistic psychology. He focused on human development through the meeting of needs and founded his system of development on what he called a hierarchy
of needs. Maslow's hierarchy of human needs begins with the foundational need
for survival and is followed by subsistence, shelter, and security. Next is affiliation,
which is followed by achievement and self esteem—leading finally to self-actualization (Maslow, 1968). Maslow identified all but his final level of existence as
survival driven. He thought self-actualization was the only level that flowed from
"being," expressing and maximizing itself. He allowed that only 2 to 5% of the
population was currently living at that level. He provides a good deal of understanding that can aid the lifelong learner. He helps you understand what you need
to maximize your development, and his model explains times when you are stuck.
For instance, you might yearn for love but, if you are obsessed with surviving from
day to day, this level of affiliation will be very challenging to develop. He points
you, the lifelong learner, to your highest self and tells you that you need to satisfy
basic needs in order to develop to higher levels.

Maslow, Graves, and Loevinger, perhaps the best researched and most tested
of these developmental theorists, all agree that most human behavior is based on
scarcity or fear, adaptation rather than expression, and avoidance rather than
seeking. The implications of this for you are to understand and recognize your
fears so you can do two things. The first is to meet your safety and developmental
needs in the fear. The second is to learn to move beyond fear to truly expressive
and even love-oriented behavior (Lee, 1999).

Of particular interest at Wright are the parallels in these great thinkers. Not
only did most see fear and scarcity as primary motivators for the majority most
of the time but inspirationally, they see people as capable of developing and learn-

ing to operate from higher perspectives and toward higher capabilities. A similar message comes from another well-known developmental thinker, Lawrence Kohlberg. It is not until his level three, stage six in moral development, that Kohlberg believes that the individual acts according to internalized ideals and is free to follow individual conscience—as opposed to submitting to the norm of the group. It takes significant moral development to stand against the group when you disagree, to act in opposition to group-accepted but personally unacceptable behaviors and norms (Kohlberg, 1984).

Most developmental thinkers describe the more highly evolved individual as free, respectful, trusting, responsible, and capable of critical thinking and acting according to their own conscience and values regardless of the reactions of others. You could say they are values-driven with a strong internal locus of control while feeling deep connectedness and integration as opposed to alienation. These can also be used as goals for your own development.

These models give us a window into levels of consciousness as they relate to and develop in individuals and societies. Most allow for some level of fixation or interrupted development resulting from genetic, circumstantial, environmental, or family deficits—the limitations of which define the individual's way of thinking, being and acting.

The basic orientation at Wright is that humans are all developing in consciousness—individuals and human society alike. The thinking of Maslow, Kohlberg, Erikson, Graves, Freud, and so many others has been critical and inspirational for their exploration of human development and mapping of your possibilities. At Wright, we believe that this area of thought is essential for the lifelong learner who is truly interested in full personal development. As the humanists are so quick to point out, self-knowledge is key to achieving the fulfillment of human potential. By mapping your consciousness you can recognize patterns, change your actions, and develop yourselves to higher levels of developmental potential. In regard to making the choices that lead to change, it is existential philosophy that provides a means of putting developmental theories into daily action.

EXISTENTIAL PHILOSOPHY

As a lifelong learner, you can benefit from many aspects of existential philosophical and psychological theory. In existential thinking, life is a conscious project of personal growth. As introduced in Chapter 1, existential philosophy has contributed greatly to our understanding of our lives as personal creations. It is seen as the most important, comprehensive creation of your life. A basic premise of existential philosophy is that you create who you are. You do this by the choices you make (Yalom, 1980). The fact of your existence precedes who you are or become, meaning that, first of all, you exist. Your essential identity flows from your existence, and existence is a process of becoming—of actualizing your possibilities by your life choices. You define yourself by these choices—by the stands you take; by what you avoid; by how you love, work, and express your being in the world.

The existential perspective calls you to be aware of each moment of your life because it is in each moment that you make the choices that define you. Without the existential perspective, you are less likely to recognize the infinite possibilities available to you at each moment. You are more likely to go about life as if it were happening to you, rather than seeing your life as a grand adventure of choice. This is the point where Adlerian and existential thinking come to agreement; Adlerians and existentialists share the concept of purposive behavior. Adlerians assume that all behavior is purposive, and many existentialists see our behavior this way, too. For the existentialist, you must take charge of your existence with conscious choices while, for Adler, you must challenge limiting beliefs to fulfill your potential and really take full charge of the life you create. You learn to recognize the moments of choice as the moments of creation of your life. In this moment-by-moment recognition, you become conscious of your role in the creation of your life and you begin to see ways to choose differently and thereby to learn and grow to your advantage. To explore the existential perspective, the following sections present the theories of the existential philosophers who have had the most profound influence on the fields of psychology and lifelong learning—Søren Kierkegaard, Friedrich Nietzsche, Martin Heidegger, and Jean-Paul Sartre.[3]

SØREN KIERKEGAARD

Existential philosophers have seen the sum of the basic choices you make and principles or basic values governing them as an integral part of what they often refer to as your life project (Medlock, 1986). As Dr. Judith Wright introduced in Chapter 1 in presenting her concept of the One Decision, Kierkegaard (1843) identified a core existential choice as the choice between an aesthetic life and an

---

[3] Dr. Robert Wright presented this material in 1992 at the First International Conference on Existential Psychotherapy with JoAnne Peterson. His coauthor, Dr. Gordon Medlock, was not present at this event (Wright, Peterson, and Medlock, 1992).

ethical life. The aesthetic is based on the pleasure principle with the seducer Don Juan as the archetype—living for the pleasure of the moment and the appreciation of the beauty of life, and then moving on to his next conquest and the further pursuit of pleasure when his interest fades. The ethical life, on the other hand, is based on the principle of commitment, with marriage as the paradigm (Kierkegaard, 1843.) The committed partner recognizes that he defines himself through his commitment to the principle of marriage, and in so doing takes on the project of being a self who is that commitment.

Kierkegaard mentions the character Don Juan as a person avoiding commitment. He exercises the principle of choice to avoid commitment. Ultimately, he lives in despair of not being a self, according to Kierkegaard. Don Juan's restless pursuit of pleasure is an attempt to cope with the underlying despair of being committed to nothing, thereby not being a full self. Kierkegaard identifies an even higher exercise of choice, the religious life, which is focused on trust or faith—the principle of trust or faith in a higher power, with the Knight of Faith being the paradigm (Kierkegaard, 1843/1983). He renounces all prospects of material good or well being with his choice to follow God's will and in so doing attains the joy of surrender to a life of higher purpose. The Old Testament story of Abraham's willingness to sacrifice his son Isaac to fulfill God's will is an example of living as a Knight of Faith.

To Kierkegaard, your life project is one of progression—from a life of pleasure to a life of commitment to a life of faith or spirituality. The life project is not simply a matter of arbitrary choices in the moment, but rather of fundamental choices contributing to how you define who you are. As lifelong learners, you can begin to get a perspective on your voyage and use this perspective to choose to reach even higher or choose to stop and rest at a lower perspective, all the time knowing that there is even more available to you.

The principle of choice—that you are responsible for creating who you are—is perhaps Kierkegaard's most important contribution to psychological theory. His analysis of the higher developmental stages of ethical and religious life is also an important precursor to developmental theory.

Choice is the existential principle by which you create yourself. It is the moment-by-moment action, thought, and feeling you opt to have in response to your world. By learning to recognize how your choices define you, you can begin to move toward a more ideal self—by choosing differently than you might choose automatically if you didn't have an awareness of the principle of choice.

FRIEDRICH NIETZSCHE

You will soon see why we at Wright believe that Nietzsche challenges and guides you to your most authentic self. Nietzsche (1895) provides an important counterpoint to Kierkegaard in that regard. He emphasizes the principles of aliveness and truthfulness as essential to your project of personal growth and sees your basic existential task as one of recovering your aliveness and vitality, which he saw as buried under the hypocrisy of Victorian morality. His "higher purpose" could be said to be aimed at exposing the hypocrisy in all such claims to "higher purpose" or morality, and he describes his own purpose as "lower"—to help us get in touch with our aliveness (Nietzsche 1889).

Nietzsche demonstrated a clear commitment that was core to his life project, the quest for truth: the truth of healthy narcissism as opposed to self sacrifice, the truth of the body (instincts and feelings) rather than the ethereal spirit, the truth of the shadow self with its socially unacceptable motivations instead of the false self of the so-called "good man." Nietzsche's life project was to overcome the lies by which he lived and face his true self. Nietzsche provides an important corrective to the joyless vision of life projected by Kierkegaard. Yet Nietzsche's work is still rooted in what the Wright model terms reactivity, with indications that he failed to address some of the important early developmental issues in his own life. By studying his life, it is possible to see how he was deeply hurt by the ingenuine behavior of those around him, and he never really became the expressive, genuine person he portrayed for us.

Aliveness, as Nietzsche identifies it, is a key principle and conceptual tool for the lifelong learner. At any moment, you can choose to be more or less alive. Our assumption is that by choosing greater aliveness, you are generating a more complete self. Aliveness can lead to commitment and faith but we do not need to become falsely pious, one of the main peeves of Nietzsche. Couple aliveness with expression of truth to your highest vision, and you harness a powerful force toward becoming the most you can be.

When we talk about the principle of truth, we are referring to your expression of the highest, deepest, or fullest truth available to you in the moment. This truth will guide you unerringly into your most authentic self. Combine truth with aliveness and you have powerful guides for your growth.

MARTIN HEIDEGGER

Authenticity and commitment are two other values to use in your life quest for your fullest self. Authenticity refers to who you truly are as opposed to the self you present to the outside world—the edited, socially acceptable self. As you narrow the gap between your socially presented self and your internal life, you become more genuine or authentic. Authenticity includes congruity, the consistence of actions, thoughts, and feelings. Do you smile when sad? If so, you are probably being incongruent.

Martin Heidegger (1927) defined the life project as one of becoming authentically who you are—the basic choice between authenticity and inauthenticity, to fulfill your own unique potential and destiny or to live according to others' expectations and social convention. You, too, can embrace this choice as a lifelong learner. The journey of life can be easily encompassed in the journey to authenticity. Living authentically, for Heidegger, involved the ability to assume responsibility for your self, the commitment to take a stand, and resoluteness in the pursuit of one's "calling," with a capacity for nonattachment or release. This release can be facilitated by a commitment or openness to pure or essential being (Zimmerman 1981).

When you, the lifelong learner, dedicate yourself to being fully present in life and serving some higher cause, your personal power, fulfillment, and development are enhanced. A key element of your life project is involved in your ability to commit and dedicate your life. Commitment is not only a value, but a principle. Commitment refers to the quality of human beings dedicating themselves and their lives to something higher or beyond their everyday concerns. One example presented previously was Nietzsche's commitment to truth in his life project.

As you fulfill your more basic commitments to be nourished and safe, you automatically develop personally and are capable of more complete commitments.

JEAN-PAUL SARTRE

Sartre's work shows that play is a key principle in your life project. Play is also the principle of "here and now" interactions between you and yourself, you and another person, or you and a thing. Play is aliveness in interaction that causes you to be nourished and to grow. Play is not necessarily amusing or pleasant. It is any interaction, pleasurable or painful, that causes you to develop. As a lifelong learner, you can enhance your journey by learning to play more fully with your world. In developing the idea of play in the service of our life project, Sartre built on Heidegger's vision of the individual's life project with his notion of the "fundamental project of being." Key elements of the project of being are a spirit of playfulness, as opposed to seriousness, and a quality of full engagement in living (Sartre, 1943).

Sartre moves beyond Heidegger as he explores the interpersonal context in which the individual undertakes the life project of personal growth, and elaborates that vision in his existential biographies, culminating in his final work on Gustave

Flaubert. Sartre, as opposed to Heidegger, appreciated the importance of childhood and family of origin patterns in defining the individual's life project, but his own limited view of relationship—a predominately narcissistic orientation to the world— and the high level of reactivity and opposition in all his work, prevented him from articulating any clear positive vision of the individual's life project. This narcissism is reflected in his analysis of concrete relations in Being and Nothingness—all relationships are characterized by objectification, sadomasochism, and alienation. There is no possibility of truly being with others, of intimacy, of authentic sharing, which are presumably bourgeois illusions for Sartre (Medlock, 1986).

BEYOND FRAGMENTATION
TO A POSITIVE INTEGRATIVE VISION

Building on the collected work of the existentialists, you find that, though there are differences across the various existential perspectives, agreement exists that your individual self is defined by a series of choices that make up your unified life project. There is also agreement that for you, the individual, to be truly yourself— to be genuine, truthful, and authentic or whole—you must separate from convention, or adherence to the comfortable, self-definitions provided by society, and undertake to define yourself as a conscious project. This includes responsibility for your life in all the aforementioned positions: a quality of commitment to principle and a sense of purpose as with Kierkegaard and Heidegger, a willingness to tell the truth fully as Nietzsche defined, and a quality of playful engagement in living as seen in Nietzsche and Sartre. There appears to be a consensus among the existentialists regarding these essentials of the individual's life project.

Although each of these existential principles has validity in and of itself, the principles can be correlated to developmental levels. As you will see in greater detail in the next chapter, there is an ascending complexity in the transformational principles of growth and development that grow from existential philosophy, beginning with aliveness as the most basic and foundational principle, continuing to play, and then intentionality. Looking at those three principles you can see that intentionality adds an element of volition. Whereas aliveness is the raw foundational principle, play can be seen as aliveness in relationship to self, others, and things. Complexity increases with the addition of volition in intentionality and continues as you see truth of your experience to your highest vision, including all of the previous stages and expanding to include an integrity and expression of self beyond intentionality. Genuineness is added to intentionality. Commitment adds yet another level of complexity as well as responsibility. Based on the work of the developmental theorists, where the individual is able to deal with increasing complexity, a rough parallel between those increasingly demanding principles and the developmental process becomes apparent.

At several of the academic conferences where Dr. Robert Wright and his colleagues presented their correlations between existential principles and developmental psychology, participants in the conferences indicated that the Wright model was the only application they had ever seen of existential principles to developmental theory. The possible exception may be Ken Wilber, although he makes the link with a different framework that is more of a combination of existential-Eastern spiritual principles and Western Developmental Psychology (Wilber, 1980). Prompted by the frequent comments of conference participants, academics, and professionals, Wright staff have searched the literature and have so far found no other evidence of models that apply existential principles to developmental theory.

As the next chapter shows, the existential principles correlate to developmental levels, as follows: Aliveness, the foundational principle, correlates to Level One, 0 to six months. Play correlates to Level Two, the period of identity formation, six months to three years. Intention correlates to Level Three, the terrible twos, extending from eighteen months through seven years of age. Truth becomes central in Level Four, conformity, where expression of truth to our highest vision is the challenge and guide for the adolescent. Commitment becomes central at Level Five for the young adult, and responsibility is the challenge at Level Six for the adult.

Adlerian psychology, developmental psychology, and existential philosophy help you understand yourself and strategize your best life in many ways. The limiting beliefs and spheres of life from Adler allow you to identify what hindrances you must overcome while giving you a method by which to clarify what you want to accomplish in different areas of your life. The developmental thinkers have aided you so that you can learn what stage of development you are in, what you need to develop further, where you are developing, what the highest level is, and what you need to do to reach it. Adding to this, the existentialists empower you by demonstrating that it is your responsibility to create the life you want to live and showing you the important principles you can use to do this. What you gain from these three schools of psychology and philosophy is a powerful and concrete foundation to help you in your quest for lifelong learning and in achieving your greatest potential.

CHAPTER THREE

THE WRIGHT MODEL OF PERSONAL GROWTH AND DEVELOPMENT

*An Applied Methodology
for Lifelong Learning*

CHAPTER THREE

THE WRIGHT MODEL OF PERSONAL GROWTH AND DEVELOPMENT

*An Applied Methodology
for Lifelong Learning*

INTRODUCTION

NOW THAT YOU ARE ORIENTED TO THE TERRAIN *in your quest for the destination of a great life, it's time to take look at the map itself. The Wright Model of Personal Growth and Development provides a detailed map that both helps you select your route and guides you on your journey to your authentic self. Although psychological and philosophical perspectives can help you reach your maximum potential, it takes more than theories and ideas to stimulate maximal growth for you as a lifelong learner. To put the ideas into action, you need to use them as a foundation for the way you operate in the world and a map that allows you to integrate them into a working model that can be followed and tested.*

As a result of the consumer research done in the 1980s, Dr. Robert Wright and his colleagues designed a comprehensive developmental model that allows you to organize, integrate, follow, and test your emerging experiences and ideas. It is a model which incorporates the Adlerian, developmental, and existential perspectives presented in Chapter 2. The Wright Model of Personal Growth and Development provides the developmental framework for the educational philosophy, methodologies, and technologies used at Wright, including Wright Performative Education and the Assignment Way of Living, described in Chapter 4.

This chapter begins with a presentation of the Wright Model of Human Growth and Development and its three axes: Consciousness, Existential, and

Relationship. Next is an explanation of developmental psychology as it applies to the model's Consciousness axis: the levels of consciousness. It continues with an explanation of existential approaches, applied as the model's Existential axis: the transformational principles. Finally, the chapter concludes with a presentation of Adlerian psychology, applied as the model's Relationship axis: the areas of life.

THE WRIGHT MODEL

THE WRIGHT MODEL OF PERSONAL GROWTH and Development consists of three axes that serve as a guide for viewing your work as a lifelong learner. You can look at it as you would at a map with a north/south axis, an east/west axis, and altitude. The north/south axis is an axis of consciousness. It consists of seven developmental levels. The east/west parallel is an axis of relationship. It maps your relationship to every area of your life, from your body, to yourself, your family, friends, work, and so on. The third axis can be likened to altitude. It is an axis of principles and choices fundamental to your living the fullest life possible.

Together, these three axes constitute a three-dimensional grid to assess growth, set goals, and help you identify and analyze problems and issues in your life, just as a map lets you figure out where you are and where you want to go. Furthermore, the model provides invaluable guidance in planning your growth and development around these goals, issues, and problems, just as a map helps you choose your route to your destination. This grid or map provides a context and focus for your developmental work at any point in your personal growth. This personal development map also allows you to identify where you are in your larger personal development process, at what you are aiming, and the steps necessary for reaching your goals (see Table 1).

DEVELOPMENTAL PSYCHOLOGY APPLIED:
LEVELS OF CONSCIOUSNESS

The model identifies seven developmental levels to help you recognize and meet developmental needs. The levels of consciousness correspond closely with the traditional developmental models, as described in Chapter 2. One major difference between Erikson's stages and the Wright model, however, is that all of these levels operate in the present, while Erikson showed them as progressing through life as

TABLE 1: *Wright Model of Personal Growth and Development*

RELATIONSHIP AXIS

CONCIOUSNESS AXIS

Level	Body	Self	Family	Groups Other	Play Work	Principles & Society	Life Purpose & Relationship to Higher Power
Consciousness (Non-Dualistic)							Transcendental Principles**
Authority vs. Superiority						Responsibility	
Purpose vs. Striving					Commitment		
Expression vs. Conformity				Truth			
Assertion vs. Reactivity			Intent				
Affirmation vs. Hunger		Play					
Trust vs. Scarcity	Aliveness*						

*Principles of identity formation operational at this and next two levels; identification, ingestion, incorporation, projection, etc

** Transcendental principles including; compassion, acceptance, love, etc.

a sequential, bi-modal challenge. Although he recognized failure as the inability to complete a level, he did not generate a model as useful and dynamic for everyday guidance. In the Wright model, each level represents an ego state. Different life circumstances activate various ego states in you, and the states vary depending on your developmental history.

These are perhaps best correlated to Eric Berne's ego states (1961). Where

Berne talks about the parent, adult, and child—which correspond to Freud's superego, ego, and id—the Wright model speaks of scarcity or trust, hunger or affirmation, reactivity or assertion, etc. These dichotomies correspond to levels of development with the hunger level relating most strongly to Freud's narcissistic period of development. The Wright model conceptualizes these states as fluid, with you revisiting them repeatedly, especially when a piece of unfinished business at one level is evoked by a challenging circumstance in which you find yourself. Changing circumstances will evoke different reactions. For example, a machine gun pointed at you might evoke scarcity whereas a strong, fatherly figure like Santa Claus might evoke safety and trust. Similarly, what looks like a rejecting look in a meeting might elicit hurt and hunger to be affirmed, and thereby indicate the need to talk and receive help and affirmation. The levels follow:

FIGURE 1: *Levels of Consciousness in the Wright Model*

Level One	*Trust*	*vs.*	*Scarcity*
Level Two	*Affirmation*	*vs.*	*Hunger*
Level Three	*Assertion*	*vs.*	*Reactivity*
Level Four	*Expression*	*vs.*	*Conformity*
Level Five	*Purpose*	*vs.*	*Striving*
Level Six	*Authority*	*vs.*	*Superiority*
Level Seven	*Consciousness (Undifferentiated)*		

Each of the first six levels consists of two poles that can be likened to the members of a stair, with the tread being the progressive, or expressive, aspect (indicated first in each pairing) and the vertical riser being the regressive, or reactive, aspect, as shown in Figure 2. Most of us have yet to meet all of the developmental requirements at each of the levels, leading us to experience psychological unfinished business as external circumstances evoke these—experiencing fear (Level One), hurt (Level Two), or anger (Level Three) in our daily lives. The psychological space in which lifelong learners typically become stuck or fixated is generally regressive.

FIGURE 2: *Levels of Consciousness and Choice*

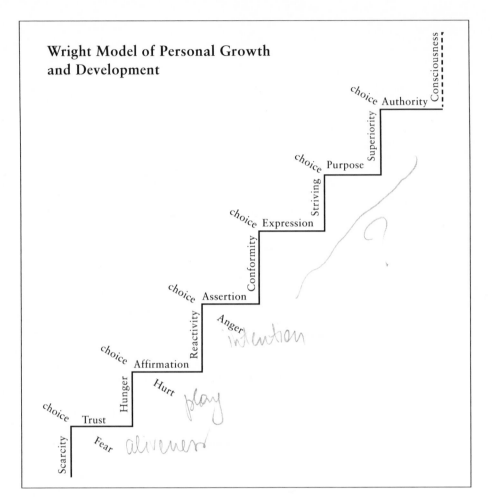

Although Erik Erikson is best known for his developmental model that appears like this at first blush, it was Vernon Woolf who created this type of bi-modal model to provide a dynamic, here-and-now analytic perspective useful to the student in guiding daily actions so that they complete unfinished business (1990). Woolf added a dynamic element to the model, improving its usefulness by adding a positive direction while maintaining the definition of the deficit. With repeated application we came to see the model as stairs—just as stairs need their vertical and horizontal members, we all need and are made up of progressive states and regressive needs which, if filled or met, add to our development. The levels can be represented in a host of ways, including rings like a tree or spirals, such as are found in the work of Graves (2002).

The progressive poles indicate movement toward advancing development or consciousness while the regressive polarities are necessary to the development and achievement of the progressive poles. They represent foundational needs and can actually represent an advance over apparently "higher" positions—an integral part of progress where two steps forward may include one step back and the stepping back facilitates a big jump forward. Over the years, experience with students has revealed that each time you advance vertically, you regress to earlier, more foundational needs.

For example, a promotion at work may result from increasing security and maturity in dealing with team member conflict; however, that very promotion evokes new emotions and unfinished business as you experience new challenges to belong while fulfilling your position of leadership. This becomes apparent in personal development when lifelong learners begin trusting an individual trainer and/or the personal development process and they regress to earlier, more elementary ego states and the needs found at those levels, such as the hunger and pain seen at Level Two. The job promotion might lead you to feel more alone. Even though you received a promotion, more primitive fears at Level One and hungers for acknowledgment at Level Two could possibly be activated. Similarly, unfinished business at Level Three and Level Four is also likely to be brought to the fore, indicating the need for further development.

Each consciousness or developmental level corresponds to a fundamental existential principle that is helpful or even essential in the individual's transition from the regressive state to the progressive state. For example, Level One, scarcity and trust, correlates to aliveness, and Level Four, conformity and expression, correlates to truth. The remainder of this chapter focuses on the parts of the Wright model, beginning with the levels of consciousness, followed by the principles, the areas of life, and finally, the mechanisms by which you operationalize the process.

Just as the existential principles facilitate the movement from the regressive to the progressive pole at each level, you will see later how each level and principle correlates to one of the Adlerian Areas of Life. First, however, you need to understand the developmental levels to see how you can use them to understand your daily reality and use this understanding to help you get more out of every day.

CONSCIOUSNESS LEVEL 1:
SCARCITY AND TRUST

This most basic level of development challenges you to move from scarcity to trust, and corresponds to the principle of aliveness. The challenge at this level is to learn to trust life and the world. Success at this stage provides a strong foundation for successful living. The ability to recognize scarcity when it operates in everyday life allows the individual to maximize development and move through difficulties that would cause others to stop or even break down.

Scarcity is a fact of life. There are conditions such as famine or poverty where there truly is not enough. There are times when lives are at risk, and scarcity is the appropriate response. In scarcity, you act to keep yourself alive. You limit your expression, or you express with the purpose of maintaining life. You respond to hostile elements in the world around you. Unfortunately, most of us, consciously or unconsciously, imagine dangers in our lives where there are none. When you don't risk in order to avoid unreal, imagined consequences, you inadvertently reduce possible adventures, and your life is limited and less satisfying as a result. By learning to trust more fully and to express in your life more fully, by taking full responsibility for your scarcity, you learn, grow, and develop your ability to trust.

The most primitive regressive pole at which you can become fixated is scarcity. Someone who operates primarily at this level is said to be operating in scarcity consciousness. Fear is the primary emotion to be integrated at this level. To the extent that your childhood world was not safe physically and emotionally, you fear expressing your full aliveness as an adult, and you hold back. In this case, you are more likely to make choices based on scarcity. A serious threat can trigger anyone into scarcity consciousness. For example, a man confronted by another who is pointing a gun at him will likely and appropriately choose scarcity consciousness as his operating mode for its inherent survival value.

Scarcity and fear become a growth issue only when they become a fixation or stuck point, where you primarily operate in that mode. When fixated at this level, you adopt a victim stance. Motivation is dominated by fear—usually fear of harm or loss, or failure to achieve a desired outcome, sometimes causing impulsive behavior and inactivity. At other times, however, in business meetings, you might be "operating out of scarcity" inappropriately and limiting your satisfaction and, ultimately, your development. In this case, by recognizing safety needs and assessing real versus imagined dangers, you can take a risk and learn to trust yourself and your world even more. However, a lifelong learner will learn to recognize scarcity and fear as restraining and will challenge the fear more often.

As scarcity is mastered, you will live with greater trust. You recognize fear, and it becomes a friend, warning you of danger and otherwise receding to a watchful distance. To some extent everyone has unfinished business at this level; however, those who do not transition sufficiently to trust during this period of childhood tend to live defensive and disturbed lifestyles. See how scarcity or lack is manifest in the regressive poles of each of the higher levels in Figure 3:

FIGURE 3: *Scarcity in the Regressive Poles of the Levels of Consciousness*

Level One	*Scarcity—of basic needs and fear of death*
Level Two	*Hunger—scarcity in attention and positive affirmation*
Level Three	*Reactivity—scarcity in being able to exercise one's will*
Level Four	*Conformity—fear of rejection by the group*
Level Five	*Striving—scarcity and urgency in life direction*
Level Six	*Superiority—scarcity in being rationalizes shortcomings*
Level Seven	*Consciousness*

Trust is the progressive pole of the first level of development. Trust is defined as having confidence in something, relying on some quality or attribute of a person or thing, or the truth of a statement (Oxford English Dictionary, 1991). In having trust in yourself, life, and the truth, you expand and grow more fully. Whereas most people understand trust as a property insuring safety, the Wright model describes trust as feeling safe while living life fully. The standard definitions of trust require limiting variables to reduce unpredictability while the Wright definition indicates self-reliance and confidence in dealing with a multiplicity of variables rather than reduction of variables. For example, Wright students aim to trust in the principle of truth, and qualities such as integrity rather than guarantees of what will not happen. They see trust in themselves and their ability to respond, rather than a guaranteed trust in limiting possible unpredictable variables. In the realm of relationship, Wright students see trust in the truth rather than the traditional idea of trust that most people have when they say that they trust that a friend will not criticize them. At Wright, we see trust in principles such as truth as a much more robust and enlivening way of being.

The ontological and epistemological implications of this are significant. Our ontology defines the human being as robust, adaptable, and ever-changing, whereas traditional perspectives see human beings as fragile, victims of circumstances, and limited in possibilities and ways of being or adapting. The epistemology to which the Wright model harkens sees humans as developing in consciousness. It similarly defines a reality of development and growth with infinite creative possibilities and positive outcomes. This stands in stark contrast to traditional epistemologies based on original sin, a guilt-based epistemology with women suffering in childbirth and men struggling to raise crops.

Simply speaking, trust relates to your confidence in your ability to respond effectively to the challenges of life. With sufficient successful experiences of trust, you can say that you have internalized trust and that you believe in the hospitality of the world. With internalized trust, you express freely when possible and protect when necessary. Trust is indicated by your ability to adapt to our world, respond effectively, and successfully express your needs. When you are born, you experience scarcity and you are vulnerable. You literally cannot live without the intervention of your parents. To the extent that they create a safe environment for you in the physical and emotional world, you learn to express your aliveness. You learn to trust the world, and the world becomes your domain.

CONSCIOUSNESS LEVEL 2: HUNGER AND AFFIRMATION

This period is the time when you are forming your core identity. Hunger is the craving to exist as an individual that causes you to seek your reflection in the world. In hunger you seek affirmation of who you are. The primary concern or question at Level One relates to who you are, how the world views you, and what you can expect from the world. The task at this level is to develop a nourished, growing sense of self or "who I am." Once your continued existence is established at Level One, at this phase your basic needs for identity are met and you develop a sense of self. This is a time of core identity formation that corresponds to ages from six months to two or three years of age. During this time your hunger for affirmation is a driving force and you soak up the world's perspective of you like a sponge. This period corresponds roughly to Freud's narcissistic period of development (English and Finch, 1964). The principle of play is especially important at this level. It is the interaction of play that causes your basic hunger needs to be met, or not. When hunger needs are met, it results in affirmation.

Interpersonally, hunger is the yearning for contact that connects us as human beings. Developmentally, hunger represents the regressive aspect of this level and affirmation is the progressive aspect. Play is the principle whereby hunger needs are expressed and sometimes met. Hunger is the predominant developmental step in the period when the developing self is in need of being reflected back with positive regard by the surrounding world, while hunger reappears psychologically, just as it does physically. Unsatisfied early or core hunger manifests in adulthood in patterns such as passive-aggressive behavior, extreme neediness, or even extreme denial of needs. As neediness it appears in highly dependent, "oral," clinging, and enmeshed relationships, often with the feeling "nothing is ever enough." When we deny our unmet hunger needs, we can appear cold, aloof, and even "schizoid" in our approach to the world and relationships. "I don't need anyone" is a typical life-position statement of someone in denial of hunger. Once recognized, chronic patterns of hunger can be responded to with changed behavior, allowing you to continue adult development where it left off in childhood, thereby enhancing the richness of daily life and creating a new, more affirming lifestyle (Morningstar, 1981).

A strong positive sense of self develops when your hunger needs are adequately met. By understanding this, you can learn to recognize your hunger needs and either meet them yourself or reach out to others for support and positive affirmation. As your hunger needs are acknowledged and met, you will develop an increasingly strong sense of self, one where you expect sufficiency in the world. You will become increasingly capable of self-affirmation in the face of challenge. Additionally, when you find yourself increasingly capable of self-affirmation you will, at the same time, develop the skills to reach out to others. Throughout life, nobody is totally self-sufficient. Everyone needs periodic reinforcement and satisfaction of hunger needs.

There are many dramatic examples of the importance of affirmation and what happens when hunger needs are chronically not met. These examples are evident in situations where there is complete deprivation of affirmation. One murderer with whom Dr. Robert Wright worked was deprived of virtually all affirmation from birth when his mother entered a psychiatric hospital, never to exit in his childhood. Absence of positive affirmation can weaken even the strongest of people.

For example, it has been documented that even the best-prepared and strongest personalities were sorely challenged in the Korean conflict as prisoners of war. This conflict saw the most devastating loss of prisoners of war, with a high suicide and death rate despite minimal deprivation of food and little physical abuse. The absolute lack of affirmation was so devastating that some prisoners simply stopped living. This was accomplished by the North Koreans who delivered only bad news to American prisoners. Prisoners were told of their compatriots' complicity with the North Koreans. Positive affirmation was strictly reserved for traitors. This vacuum of affirmation was a major element in causing significant breakdown and even death in thirty percent of the prisoners so deprived (Rath & Clifton, 2004).

On the other hand, when hunger needs are met, the result is a growing, increasing ability to affirm yourself, even in the face of direct disaffirmation. Affirmation refers to your ability to see yourself objectively and accept yourself, thereby affirming your existence and accepting the truth of what and who you are. Affirmation refers to having your needs met, being seen and perceived with positive regard, knowing you exist, knowing who you are, and knowing that you are okay. Hunger is the lack of affirmation and the need to be seen. Hunger in your body is the sign that you need to be fed while hunger in your psyche likewise indicates a need for nourishment.

As these needs are met during your initial development, you develop a sense of self. In the ideal, you are reflected back to yourself with unconditional positive regard, accurately reflecting what is going on with you in the here-and-now. This accurate, unconditional reflection creates a positive sense of self, often leading to what is referred to as high or positive self-esteem. In adulthood, most of you have some level of hunger remaining from childhood and during the remainder of your life you can incrementally build that which was not built. Be it in singlehood, marriage, parenting, friendship, or work, you are interacting in ways that provide opportunities to continue to be nourished and affirmed with awareness and application.

As a child develops and learns to trust, he progresses to a point of being able to interact with others in trust or hunger. He automatically begins to express his needs in the world around him and develops the ability to interact with this world. The infant is developing a personality, an identity, and a sense of being which can include a self-image that is positive or negative. Whether you develop a positive or negative self-image depends upon how the world responds to your natural hunger because, at this phase as a child, you are hungry for affirmation and see what the world reflects back to you as what you really are. Just as you look in the mirror to see yourself, that child looks into the world around him to find out what his identity is.

In lifelong learning, you seek to identify and accept your hungers. You aim to take responsibility for these hungers by expressing them and receiving affirmation from the outside when you are not capable of giving it to yourself. As you are affirmed and nourished, you have an ever-increasing wealth of affection and attention to give back to the world around you. You believe that your ability to serve and meet the needs of those who touch you is directly proportional to your ability to have your own needs met. This way you learn, grow, and are nourished.

You see yourself as being fully responsible for your own nourishment and affirmation. And to the extent that you express your hunger fully and are affirmed, you internalize that affirmation and can increasingly carry it with you. You can affirm yourself in the absence of direct affirmation from the world around you. This allows you to move increasingly into difficult areas in your life, to go for long periods of time without direct affirmation, to reach for your highest vision, to engage in a worthwhile life quest. The result is that you serve society fully and live in a more loving, supportive, just, equitable, and truthful world. You live a life that you respect and increasingly identify with your positive self. You learn to live from that positive self and learn to recognize hunger and express it responsibly as you live a playful life of ever-increasing affirmation and nourishment.

CONSCIOUSNESS LEVEL 3:
REACTIVITY AND ASSERTION

Formation of the individual identity takes a turn at Level Three. Here the identity is not only being formed by, "Who am I?" but also by a resistance to others, defining the self by what you resist. This is the period of life often referred to as the "terrible twos." During this period you are developing boundaries. To a great extent, you are defining who you are by asserting your will and resisting. The challenge at this stage is to learn to assert your will in both creative desire and resistance. It results in a profound sense that "my life is mine, and I am the creator."

At the level of assertion, you are expressing intentions and learning to assert your will.

Intention can be defined as play with direction; where play is aliveness in relationship, intention can be seen as aliveness in desire. Intention is the principle whereby you create the world around you, and assertion is the final result. Assertion is the expression of positive desire. Reactivity, on the other hand, is the regressive aspect of assertion, the more primitive foundation. In reactivity, you respond to the world around you by resisting. This is in contrast to assertion. With assertion you act on the world around you out of desire. Assertion is creation; it is expression of desire and intention in a positive way. Reactivity is negating in nature. It is an attempt to limit, an attempt to stop things.

Reactivity is an essential and often unrecognized element of your experience in daily life. In daily life, reactivity is integrated and often undifferentiated so you find it difficult to recognize. In laboratory learning situations in lifelong learning, we expect reactivity in lab members. We also expect members to develop the ability to recognize and acknowledge reactivity, to discover its positive intention, to recognize the need behind it, to meet that need, and ultimately, to harness that intention with an increasing capacity for assertion and conscious creation in their lives. We support students to openly acknowledge responsibility for reactivity, while developing a clean and powerful assertion.

Reacting requires something against which we react. Here, the individual is defining him or herself by that against which they react. Will is being forged and, if not squashed or shamed, a strong sense of personal power can result with the individual becoming more assertive than reactive. Reactivity is characterized by a very strong investment in the here-and-now, resistance to control, and expression of the desire to possess and do what one wants to do. The will is being established in this phase.

There are times in your life when reactivity is an absolutely necessary skill. Failure of the world to react to Hitler's aggression caused an enormous tragedy in World War II. The failure of parents to set appropriate limits for their children can lead to a child out of control. Likewise, the failure of countries to assert positive values can lead to less than the most uplifting society possible.

Parents often have difficulty with this stage of development when this seemingly sweet and loving child enters what is called the "terrible twos." It is a difficult period for parents and children to negotiate. It is difficult because parents need to set limits while simultaneously encouraging their children to express themselves and assert their will.

At this point, it is easy to squash children's wills, and overrun their attempts to assert themselves. Children naturally intend to get things, to go places, and to stop things. The more they succeed and learn to impact their world, the more they affirm their ability to live with conscious positively directed intention. It is important to align with this principle at all levels. If children do not learn to express their intention and assert their will, it will be difficult for them as adults to feel that their world is something of their creation, an extension of their own will.

Reactivity in young children is characterized by a strong investment in the here-and-now. Resistance to control reigns as the child engages in expression of the desire to possess and do what he wants to do. The will is being established at this phase. This is also the period during which we speak of a person's will being broken. This happens when resistance is shamed or crushed with an abuse of power. In this case, conscious choice diminishes and covert desires take over.

When the reactivity of the terrible twos gets crushed in childhood, the ability to assert one's desires in adulthood becomes limited: The adult can be stuck in reactivity where he is either consistently agreeable or openly disagreeable. In either case, he does not directly or creatively assert his will. He does not believe that his life can be a positive expression of his desires. It evolves into either active or passive aggression.

Completion of reactivity sees individuals move toward assertiveness. You express your will fully. You accept logical consequences and adapt your behavior.

You do all of this while maintaining the sense that your life is the result of your own authorship and creation. We see this as the mature manifestation of aggression—the primal human drive to take things to oneself and to push away painful stimulus. Your life is yours.

Aggression matures into assertion as you grow and assimilate into society. You learn to control impulses and drives and to develop the ability to assert your will in an integrative, functional way to those around you. You learn to live in "expression of" rather than in "opposition to" your reactivity. Assertion is compromised when aggression is suppressed, causing the individual to feel alienated from others.

In adulthood, failure to develop sufficient assertiveness leads to passive aggression, passive dependent, and other limiting lifestyles. To be sure, you are all learning to be more assertive in some way. This is a key part of the adventure of adulthood, even when you are also learning to let things be. Being, doing, acting, and accepting are all more readily learned in adulthood with a firm developmental foundation at this level.

CONSCIOUSNESS LEVEL 4: CONFORMITY AND EXPRESSION

Conformity and expression characterize the period extending into adolescence and beyond for most of the population. It is a time of differentiating from the family and learning to belong to the group. The challenge is to express your self while belonging to the group. According to G. M. Durst (1982), 70% of the population works to negotiate belonging and expression. At most only 30% of the population develops significantly beyond this stage. The challenge is to belong and feel accepted, while expressing yourself fully and genuinely. This is very complex and demanding challenge. Conformity is at the regressive end of the spectrum at this level, and expression is the progressive pole. This level is intimately tied into the principle of truth.

Conformity is the desire to belong. It is the act of changing our behavior to fit the group in order to experience acceptance and belonging. Expression is the full assertion of your will and the projection of yourself. Expression takes place when you express the truth of your experience to your highest vision. It takes place when you stand for your beliefs even in opposition to the group to which you belong. Truth is the principle of intentionality in a relationship. It is play and aliveness in their purest form, the expression of the self in relationship to others.

In Durst's research (1982), 80% of the population today fails to express the truth of their experience to their highest vision in day-to-day life. Fear of rejection, losing jobs, reprisal, guilt, etc., causes you to shut down and hold back expressing your truth. This leaves you mired in the regressive aspect of this level: conformity. In conformity, your desire to belong is stronger than your desire to express. You are not allowed to say what is true for you. Nevertheless, conformity is a necessary stage of development. Ideally, as you become increasingly more and more secure in your identity and your ability to get along, you increasingly develop the ability to express the truth of your experience. This is the progressive aspect of truth.

Developing adolescents foster the urge to leave the home, to create "my own life." The developing person goes against family morals by experimenting. This reaction or rebellion is an important part of personalizing your values. You join the group for support in your separation from your family. Heavy reliance is placed on membership in the group. A desire to belong is so strong that individuality is submerged. The fear of looking different, of rejection, predominates. Expression of experience is submerged for the support of belonging. Expression of a full range of feelings and thoughts is generally withheld because conforming to the group is of utmost importance.

The definition of "conform" that informs the Wright model is, "To make one's self like . . . to bring oneself into conformity, adapt oneself . . . In such a way as to limit genuine expression of and development of the self." In general, "conformity" refers to adapting to the group. The packaging conforms to the contents in a vacuum-wrapped product. Similarly, in the conformity stage, adolescents tend to conform to their peer group. Approval of the group replaces approval of the parent.

In adolescence, this desire to belong poses a major challenge to the expression of truth with respect to your highest vision. You become stuck in conformity. At first, conformity gives you a sense of belonging, which helps you leave the family. It helps you continue on your path of independence, leading ultimately to adult interdependence. It gives you an identity outside of the family. It allows you to belong to a peer group within which you can rebel against and test parental values, thereby developing your own values. If you do not have a strong enough foundation of parental values, this test leads to a repression of self. You fail to begin expressing yourself more fully. You fail to express the truth of your experience to your highest vision. You live out of contact with your innermost knowledge and acceptance of what is real and genuine about yourself. You fail to exercise and express your judgments, emotions, likes, dislikes, desires, and motivations.

The desire to belong can occasionally be so great that identity may be sacrificed in order to have that belonging; however, because it is a force of false belonging, the benefits of truly belonging are never available. By not expressing criticisms in order to belong, for instance, you may be accepted, but you really are not being accepted because you have masked or withheld your true feelings. Conversely, the desire to belong may be strongly denied and need to be worked through. The denial of the desire to belong and the submersion of self for the sake of being included are both aspects of conformity.

Lifelong learning supports full expression of your truth. You move from conformity to full expression by expressing truth to your highest vision. Expression in this sense relates to living in accordance with your deepest self and your highest intentions. It is the progressive aspect of developmental Level Four. As children develop and firmly establish their ability to assert their will, they begin to differentiate from family and identify with their peer group. Again, this comes into focus particularly in latency and adolescence, when belonging to the group is of utmost importance. In the expressive ideal, however, once an adolescent feels secure in their identity outside the family and in the group, their next challenge is to express themselves fully, even when doing so may require them to be in opposition to the will of the group.

Expression operates from birth. Yet at the Level Four stage of development, expression calls forth a sense of self that is full enough to be called expression of self. People who have not substantially moved from conformity to expression live unconsciously in great fear of looking different from the group. The unconscious fear of rejection, ridicule, and not fitting in runs their behavior. They may even consider themselves rebels, because on the surface they have chosen a rebellious lifestyle. However, the desire to be accepted as individuals is great. The rebellion is more a function of reactivity to family, society, and the group rather than a full expression of self. Expression of self, versus reactivity, is seen when the individual is choosing to create experience in life as opposed to avoiding experience in life.

Commitment to this expression leads to broad, purposeful direction in life. This commitment is supported by meaningful daily activities and expressions. When you act with commitment to expression you know what you want and act toward that end. Furthermore, you want not only your own fulfillment, but also the success of the groups to which you belong. If you can continue to express your truth to your highest vision, the group can minister and contribute more fully to your needs. Conformity then moves into self-expression. It provides the increased sense of security that permits saying "No," going against group decisions, and risking rejection. Security in belonging while withstanding a certain amount of disapproval—yet still being able to feel okay about it and yourself—becomes a possibility.

Indeed, if you remember that each regressive pole includes the previous poles, you can see how the hunger to be seen can lead to the hunger to belong.

You can also see this as scarcity in relationship to groups, and you see how fear of fully and authentically being yourself is often at the root of, and possibly essential to, conformity; it is necessary for the progressive pole to be attained in order to experience expression of self. In conformity, you act on your need of the group with a two-sided result: to compromise as well as to become yourself. The challenge at this stage is to conform and at the same time become secure enough to express yourself as genuinely different.

As a lifelong learner, the onus is on you to learn to recognize when you are compromising your most genuine self in order to belong. You must learn to reveal yourself increasingly in the course of everyday life. You cannot correct an impasse at conformity with a single violent act. Rather, it is an adventure of unfolding and revealing your true self, even to yourself.

CONSCIOUSNESS LEVEL 5:
STRIVING AND PURPOSE

This level challenges you to commit or strive toward goals or ideals. The phase resolves itself in a sense of purpose: living life with meaning. A significant part of normal development, striving indicates the early stages of the individual moving to be all that he can be. It is characterized by bigger-is-better thinking. It may manifest as moral striving, to be the best morally, or financial striving. Regardless, there is a sense of being driven by unseen forces. It can appear as a work addiction, obsession with guilt, or perfectionism. There is an urgency to achieve, and goal fulfillment is never good enough. Relationships are seen primarily as a means to an end. Commitment is the principle that relates to this level.

Striving frequently overlays reactivity, hunger, and scarcity. Striving's "bigger-is-better" component is seen as a solution to hunger, yet it is never enough. Unlimited success does not provide a sense of fulfillment and affirmation as long as individuals do not feel okay with their needs. For example, financial success will not satisfy deep-seated feelings of scarcity when you do not believe there is enough caring and nourishment to go around.

As you strive fully, you see the hollowness in the driven state. Striving coupled with commitment completes itself naturally. A more balanced perspective on life ensues as striving changes to a strong sense of purpose and meaning. The roots in this purpose are found in the commitment to the goals of striving. Meaning is achieved either by accomplishing those goals or by seeing limitations to the goals and adjusting them. It may even mean abandoning them all together. Commitment leads to broad purposeful directions in life. These directions are supported by meaningful daily activities and expressions. When you act with commitment you know what you want and work toward that end. The result is meaning and purpose.

CONSCIOUSNESS LEVEL 6:
SUPERIORITY AND AUTHORITY

Having lived with purpose, you advance to the point where you understand more than most people. You now hold a position in which you can serve others. The challenge at this level is to take full responsibility for the gaps between stated ideals and actual behavior. You live with authority by doing so. You become fully responsible for yourself.

Responsibility is the principle whereby you create your reality. Its regressive aspect is superiority. Having lived with purpose, you learn more from others and can elevate yourself above others. Superiority is regressive because you only feel good in relationship to others and not as an independent. In superiority, you spend more time focusing on the failure of others than on developing yourself. Once superiority is lived with enough responsibility, you move to the progressive aspect. This aspect is authority.

The principle of responsibility carries you from superiority to authority. Responsibility causes you to claim the gap between ideals and behavior as your own creation. You cease blaming or making excuses and see yourself as the author of your own existence; there is no longer anyone to blame. You narrow the gap between your behavior and your stated ideals by living with authority. You do so in order to move closer and closer to living with full consciousness in connection to the source of all life.

Wright courses are intended to support individuals in learning to live with increasing authority and responsibility. The goal is promoting progress as much as possible on the path to consciousness and union. At Wright, we set this goal so that we may serve our world in the way appropriate for us as fully as possible.

Superiority is generally defined in terms of superior rank, dignity, or official status; superior or supreme command; position or authority as a superior (Oxford English Dictionary, 1991). In the Wright model, superiority further means superiority in relationship to others as an attitude or ego state where deeper hunger to be affirmed and belong is often denied. In a state of superiority, you hold yourself as superior attitudinally, rather than positionally. The quality of being superior to others denies your commonality and covers deeper insecurities. At this level of superiority and authority, you live with purpose and direction in life and know you are in a position to contribute to the world. It is in this state that many people often find that their contribution to others is actually an attempt to avoid dealing with the pain of their own unfinished business in scarcity, hunger, and reactivity.

Consciousness and the practice of expressing the truth to its highest vision promote a gradual–sometimes sudden–acceptance of frailties. This fosters the move from superiority into authority. From the position of authority you can acknowledge, take full responsibility for, and work with scarcity, hunger, reactivity, and other regressive needs. It is important to recognize the traps of superiority. Otherwise, scarcity, hunger, and reactivity all become covered by the need to know and to look good. Feeling superior and attacking others can become a mental habit or mood addiction as a way to try to feel worthy at others' expense.

The progressive pole to superiority is authority. Authority is generally defined as "the power or right to enforce obedience; moral or legal supremacy; control over, or the right to command, or give an ultimate decision" (Oxford English Dictionary, 1991). In the Wright model, the word refers to the responsible authoring of your life. Authority is a life stage in which you take full responsibility for the results you create in your life. Operating out of a sense of authority indicates a high degree of purposeful living with clear principles and ideals. You live very closely to those ideals when you have achieved authority in life. Authority creates the ability to take responsibility for discrepancies between ideals and actual behavior. The discrepancy here is less than at earlier levels because full responsibility is taken for any gap between actual behavior and stated ideals.

Authority issues block many people's development. The belief that your own satisfaction cannot be attained when negotiating situations with authority figures is a hallmark of authority issues. You assume, consciously or unconsciously, that those in authority will not want your well-being along with the fulfillment of the authority's intent. Individuals with authority issues usually fall into two categories:

1. resistive and rebellious
2. submissive and passive

The foundational belief of each category is the same: authority is not interested in their well-being but only in its own agenda. Rebellion and reactivity characterize the first style. Submission and a sense of futility comprise the second. Standing up to authority, assertion of will, and negotiating win/win solutions ___ it the group and self are all part of the education and growth process. ___ ging and overcoming authority issues, students learn to identify wants ___ They become able to ask for things, express aggression, and rebel fully. ___ ns despite the difficulty for the student to feel strong enough to assert their will with authority and come to a harmonious, aligned understanding without having negotiated a full rebellion. Authority issues are resolved more easily when earlier hunger, affirmation, scarcity, and assertion issues have been addressed.

CONSCIOUSNESS LEVEL 7:
CONSCIOUSNESS (NON-DUALISTIC)

At this level, you transform into a living example of your ideal. The Wright model does not pretend to map this level. The principles that come into play here are transcendental. They go beyond the values incorporated at each of the consciousness levels and include compassion, acceptance, and love. We call these principles transcendental because they transcend the simple dynamics of the other principles. Most people see them as religious. Although that may be true, the Wright model is concerned with their highly abstract nature. They transcend daily operation and require or encompass more than any one of the transformational principles. Love, for example, can be seen as a composite of the transformational principles. You cannot have love without aliveness, play, intent, truth, commitment, and responsibility.

EXISTENTIAL APPROACHES APPLIED:
PRINCIPLES

The Wright Model of Personal Growth and Development identifies three types of principles: developmental, transformational, and transcendental. Developmental principles are those that play a key role in identity formation. These include ingestion, identification, incorporation, and projection. Transformational principles cause you to develop toward your most responsible self. Some transcendental principles are compassion, acceptance, love, God, and forgiveness. In the view of the Wright model, the transcendental principles are founded on, or are more mature manifestations of, the transformational principles. For example, without a clear understanding of play, truth, and aliveness, concepts such as love will confound rather than clarify and give direction.

Figure 4 shows the seven transformational principles and how they correlate to the developmental levels:

FIGURE 4: *Transformational Principles Mapped to Levels of Consciousness*

Aliveness	*Level One*	*Trust/Scarcity*
Play	*Level Two*	*Affirmation/Hunger*
Intention	*Level Three*	*Assertion/Reactivity*
Truth	*Level Four*	*Expression/Conformity*
Commitment	*Level Five*	*Purpose/Striving*
Responsibility	*Level Six*	*Authority/Superiority*
Transcendental	*Level Seven*	*Consciousness*

The transformational principles are ordered in developmental sequence, ranging from the most simple and concrete to the most complex and abstract. They are illustrated using the "stairstep" metaphor in Figure 5.

Figure 5: *Transformational Principles, Levels of Consciousness, and Choice*

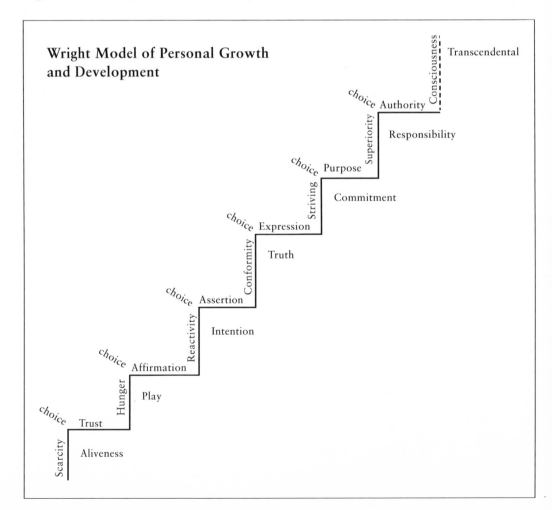

The following sections explain each transformational principle:

Aliveness

Level 1 scarcity leads to trust when you allow yourself to be more alive. Following aliveness requires trust. As you trust and allow yourself to be more alive, you develop from scarcity. You have seen how aliveness is the ultimate or foundational principle on which all other principles are founded. It is the animating principle, the principle without which there would be no life. Aliveness is your life flow. When it operates fully, you experience emotions in a fluid, full manner. This facilitates your contact with the world. It allows you to touch and be touched. Aliveness powers the other principles and is the dynamic behind them all.

Deadness is the polarity to aliveness. In deadness, you choose to withhold rather than express. In deadness, you let unfounded fears determine your choices. With aliveness you often turn fear into enthusiasm and excitement. In order to live life fully, you must learn to recognize your fears and face them. You learn to distinguish real fears that should be heeded from unreal or imagined fears that should be overcome. By learning to follow your aliveness, you automatically take the appropriate steps on the journey towards full, conscious, and responsible adulthood.

This represents a new way of being in the world. In the new way of being, you seek to live a vibrant vital life. You accept deadness as one of your human frailties to be recognized and examined. You identify the fears behind deadness, sort them out, face the unrealistic fears that are holding you back on life's journey, and move on. Just as the car needs brakes and an accelerator, each principle has its place. Unbounded aliveness could lead to an early death for most children; likewise, resistance or stopping—unbalanced by aliveness—leads to unnecessary suffering and limitation. The principle of balance requires that you be able to recognize when you are out of balance and adjust. Your ability to make adjustments is governed by your mastery of the principles.

It is possible to experience a distorted flow of aliveness—undirected, unbalanced, containing pain, joy, or hysterical reactions. Fear and pain, along with the desire to keep those feelings submerged, may cause you to suppress and compromise your aliveness. When this happens you cannot experience joy fully. The degree to which you limit pain in your life is the degree to which you also limit joy. Focusing on aliveness as a lifelong learner enables you to increase your expression of it. You learn to be more effective in that expression, and increase your internal experience.

Play

Play causes your hunger needs in Level Two to be satisfied. With play, you develop affirmation. Play occupies a central role in children's lives and provides rich opportunities to learn, grow, and develop. Human beings learn and grow more effectively from a playful relationship to what they are doing. Societal attitudes towards play are often questionable as demonstrated by such expressions as "don't play around," "you're just playing around," or "you're just playing with me." These describe a negative attitude towards the act of playing. Becoming an adult appears synonymous with ceasing to play. Work tends to be seen as drudgery rather than a type of play.

In the Wright model, play is a complete engagement in the here-and-now; complete engagement with whatever it is you are doing. This happens in such a way that you are nourished and able to grow from that interaction. Be it with something external or in relationship to themselves, those with playful attitudes find life exciting, engaging, challenging, nourishing, and fulfilling. Play is an essential principle in creation.

Lives not guided by the play principle tend to be heavy. Behaviors and fulfillment become limited and often determined by the need to avoid mistakes rather than to create desired outcomes. Play is critical in changing these attitudes. It is also a primary task for the lifelong learner. Experimentation, allowance for mistakes, and spontaneity are encouraged. Learning to engage with the world in a fully expressive and playful way enhances their ability to engage with and be engaged by the world around.

As a lifelong learner, play is an important principle for you to exercise: play sessions may be scheduled as an opportunity to learn and grow. Your learning experience, although painful, sad, and scary at times, should take place in a playful context open to growth. Seek to interact with wholeness and use play to make your life a creative process. Heeding this advice will increase the meaning of each moment of your days.

Intention

Intention is the existential principle that helps your reactive Level One needs complete themselves in assertion. Intention is first seen when children begin interacting with the world—wanting to grab and wanting to push away. This comes strongly into focus when they learn to say "No." It has been difficult for them to assert their will until this point, because they have been protected and nourished in a more womb-like atmosphere. An important concept for them to express is "No," the point where they learn to have an impact on their world. They are pushing themselves away and setting limits. They are developing volition, a strong will that manifests desires and intent.

Intentionality, when expressed appropriately, allows you to assert your will positively and creatively. Inappropriately expressed, it turns inward and the best you can do is thwart others. Life shifts from being one of expression, contribution, growth, and development to being one of survival, scarcity, and conflict. Intention becomes covert and limiting. Paradoxically, this conflict phase is necessary for adult development and in increasing the ability to be in partnership with those around you and society at large.

It is still unclear whether intention operates toward the fulfillment of conscious goals and positive direction or if it fuels resistance and suffering. The basic operational assumption in the Wright model is that individuals intend what they experience. The assumption honors human beings as powerful creators. It honors them as learning, growing entities, as they become increasingly conscious and responsible throughout the life cycle.

In lifelong learning, you assume that each of your experiences in life has an infinite number of possible responses. You therefore choose your actions by the force of your intentions. The choice is to act whereby you behave as the creator of your life. Even in the worst of conditions—being in prison, lying in bed dying of cancer, even in a time of war—choice is available to you. Even though your choices may be limited, there is still infinite possibility for you to create a life of ultimate fulfillment and satisfaction. The skill that you seek to develop is one of creating your life with increasingly conscious intention.

Truth

Conformity at Level Four progresses to expression as you learn to express the personal truth of your experience to your highest vision. Truth is the principle of intentionality in relationship. It is play and aliveness in genuine interaction in their purest forms; it is the expression of a developed self in relation to others. A large portion of the population today fails to express the truth of their experience to their highest vision in everyday life. Fear of rejection, losing a job, and other kinds of loss, cause you to shut down and hold back in expressing your highest truth. This leads to the polarity of truth, which is deception. In its purest form, truth is a full complete expression. Its fear-based polarity causes you to deceive, to hide yourself from the world around you. You keep yourself ultimately from yourself. Deception leads to aloneness.

Expressing the truth of your experience is a very complex skill and requires practice. In adolescence, you face a major challenge of expressing truth to your highest vision. Your desire to belong in a peer group places you in a bind. Can you express your desire to belong with the group of your peers and, at the same time, acknowledge your differences and your disagreements? Can you be yourself and belong? Expression of your truth to your highest vision reveals your innermost self. It requires self-knowledge and acceptance of what is real and genuine about yourself: your judgments, emotions, likes and dislikes, and desires and motivations. Telling the truth may sometimes be painful, enraging, or joyful but it almost always leads to more aliveness and clarity in relationships. You obtain security in belonging and withstanding a certain amount of disapproval, and still being able to feel okay becomes possible. You become a valuable group member while expressing yourself fully and honestly.

If you can continue to express truth toward your highest vision, it will guide, contribute, and minister to you. As a result, you can contribute more fully to the group. In our training and courses at Wright, we teach lifelong learners to express the truth toward their highest vision while expecting that they move from conformity to full expression in the process. It is our intention to develop the most full mature individual expression possible. We assume that as individuals express themselves toward their vision they elevate themselves and ultimately create the greatest contribution to the world around them.

Commitment

The existential principle of commitment causes you to develop from striving to purposeful actions at Level Five. Commitment is the expression of truth in dedication of your fully developing self toward some goal or object outside of yourself. Commitment to your goals and objects of striving causes you to learn and ultimately to live with more purpose and meaning. You develop an increasing ability to align with life, and you also develop an increasing ability to be a blessing to the environment in which you find yourself.

The polarity of commitment is avoidance. In avoidance, the fear of failure and sometimes the fear of success cause you to stop on the journey of life. You no longer keep moving in a direct path over the landscape. Instead you begin circling, avoiding, living the same problems over and over, rather than experiencing new and refreshing challenges. Your life becomes increasingly burdensome. You dedicate yourself to proving that you are not responsible for your life rather than following your commitment. You fear to risk failure and fail to learn to be increasingly masterful in your existence.

Commitment leads to broad and purposeful direction in life. Commitments are supported by and result in meaningful daily activities and expressions. When you act with commitment, you know what you are aiming at, and you work toward that end. For you, as a lifelong learner, it is useful, if not necessary, to commit your life to higher purposes in order to maximize the service you give and the return you receive on your life investment. At Wright, we support our students in fulfilling their positive life commitments. We expect them to support others in doing the same.

Responsibility

Responsibility is the principle at Level Six that moves you from superiority to authority in your life. Responsibility is a central concept borrowed from existential traditions. It describes the ability to acknowledge total authorship of your experience in life. Confusing responsibility with blame may be the greatest barrier to the assumption of responsibility. From a good-bad, right-wrong dualistic perspective on life, blame plays a major role when things do not go according to plan. Often people who blame themselves are seen as being responsible. This can be a highly limiting position. Emphasizing blame can keep you from squarely facing what is happening and engaging in it. Blame of others—and self-blame—direct energy away from accepting responsibility and toward a diversion of accountability.

Learning to take full responsibility is a major goal in personal development. Full responsibility closes the gap between your ideals and the way you really live. It increases your sense of freedom and ability to engage in full partnership with the world. It is the last of the transformational principles, leading to the transcendental principles.

Transcendental Principles

In closing and to reiterate, transcendental principles include compassion, acceptance, love, God, and forgiveness. These manifest as more mature, non-dualistic forms of the transformational principles. In the Wright model and in our courses and training, we do not use them because they generally have garnered a good deal of personal baggage over the years for students. For example, love in practice generally means more what you will not do than what you will do. You will not judge, hurt others' feelings, etc. At Wright, we assume that learning the transformational principles is a path to learning to live the transcendental principles. Take love. Can you have love without aliveness, play, intention, truth, commitment, and responsibility? You could even say that the transcendental principles are training in loving, without the baggage of childhood.

ADLER APPLIED: LIFE AREAS

Alfred Adler divided the universe of human experience into areas or spheres of existence from work to family and intimacy, as discussed previously. Within these spheres, human behavior is more easily understood. Understanding yourself, other people, and the world is also a concern of existential philosophy. In creating the Wright model, we developed a set of categories that attempt to encompass the full range of human experience and issues. This system provides a context for lifelong development work, called the life quest at Wright.

The Wright model draws from Adler and expands these divisions into seven "life areas." As described earlier, lifelong learners at Wright initially use these life areas as a structure to organize their transformation work and define areas of focus and important unfinished business. They develop a vision of a desired outcome in each of these seven life areas. For example, learners may wish to work on what is often called self-esteem. This is seen primarily in the area of self and secondarily in relationship to family and body. In various courses, the learner develops a vision of how they would like to operate, an assessment of how they currently operate, and a strategy to achieve the desired state. These elements are later used to assess progress and adjust strategies.

Life areas are arrayed in such a way that each brings to focus or relates primarily to a specific level of consciousness. Expanding on the example of self esteem, the area of self, the second area of the revised Adlerian relationship axis following body and preceding family/intimacy, relates to Level Two of the Wright model: hunger/affirmation, which follows Level One, scarcity/trust, and precedes Level Three, reactivity and assertion. The area of body/expression brings to focus the developmental issues of trust/scarcity, while family/intimacy relates directly to reactivity/assertion. This does not imply that each developmental level is expressed only in one of the life areas. It does, nevertheless, indicate a primary relationship between the level and life area, each of which is briefly described below.

The Wright model identified two dynamics that are central to body and expression: the ability to express and the ability to receive. As learners develop in this area, they increase their ability to express a wide range of feelings and thoughts. Similarly, they learn to receive or listen to a much wider range of impulses from the outside world. Their sensitivity increases and their ability to make increasingly fine distinctions becomes much more robust. The ability to be fully alive and vibrant in the body and to tune into it for information is a basic competency in this area. The primary questions here include the traditional questions of strength, flexibility, and aerobic fitness. Yet it does not necessarily deal with appearance ideals because few bodies are perceived as ideal. More central to this area is the question: to what extent does the body support your higher purpose, allow you to touch and be touched by the world, give you pleasure, and provide critical information by which you may lead your life? This perspective allows even severely handicapped individuals to engage in this question.

The relationship with the self area includes the whole array of issues and competencies associated with intrapsychic work, including inner-child work. In this area, it is important for lifelong learners to develop an unfolding awareness of their internal processes in order to maintain an increasingly nourishing, supportive, effective relationship with them. Internal strategies include the ability to recognize mistaken beliefs and ineffective internal processes and correct them. They also include knowing when to appropriately use interventions.

Family of origin work supports the development of full expression in the face of disapproval and rejection and clarification of responsibility and boundaries. In this area, it is important for students to learn how to engage in conflict and emerge having learned, grown, and become closer to the other person in the conflict. This often involves getting current and honest with family, separating and individuating, redefining family rules of communication, and establishing mutually respectful relationships. It frequently includes dealing with early traumas.

The life area of relationships with others addresses creating mutually supportive, honest, and intimate partnerships in work, play, and love. The ideal generally includes having a committed friendship network which supports one in one's higher purpose. Other aspects of the ideal relationship include the ability to give and receive support, to grow through and resolve conflict, and engage in fulfilling mutual commitment with others.

Work and play support balance in life, the quality of playfulness in work, and the ability of work to support the well-being of self and others. From this perspective, work becomes "play for pay". It represents something to which you commit that contributes to the world. It becomes an act that causes you to be nourished and to grow.

The principles/life purpose area includes clarifying life purpose and values, defining what you stand for and what principles you live by, and relating your life to the context of humanity. Higher power/spirituality involves stepping further into the process of clarifying life purpose and values. This includes defining ultimate life concerns for yourself and the planet. Principles/life purpose also engages the idea of relationship to the ultimate ground of being or higher power (God). Finally, it moves you into living a life totally dedicated to the higher, transcendental, principles of love, grace, acceptance, and unity.

Each life area defines a content focus for development or personal growth work. As a lifelong learner, you may enter personal growth coaching or trainings as a result of a relationship problem with a spouse. In the course of that work, you may address issues regarding relationship with some or all of the seven life areas. At any point, using this framework, you can define the primary and secondary content areas. Lifelong learners are encouraged to develop ideals in each of the life areas. Personal growth coaching or training is a process of developing these ideals and learning to live toward them. It is a process to increase capacity, to make choices in consonance with the stated ideals.

CHAPTER FOUR

WRIGHT PERFORMATIVE EDUCATION

*Theoretical Foundations and
Educational Methodologies
for Lifelong Learning*

CHAPTER FOUR

WRIGHT PERFORMATIVE EDUCATION

Theoretical Foundations and Educational Methodologies for Lifelong Learning

INTRODUCTION

MAPS WORK VERY WELL ON THEIR OWN. *Guidebooks that show you how to make the most of the journey are even better. This chapter gives you specific tools that make your journey into your potential more than a trip you remember fondly after the fact. These tools allow you to make real, lasting changes; they form the methodology developed at Wright that shows you how to lead a great life, a life guided by healthy desires leading to emotional and spiritual fulfillment—a life we call the life of More. In this chapter, Dr. Judith Wright presents the theoretical foundations of Wright's teaching technology, along with the practical application and impact of these on our students and their respective spheres of influence.*

Research increasingly shows that equally as important as the depth, breadth, and relevance of the curricular content to students' success, is the teaching methodology and learning technology. How you learn has a significant effect on the success of what you learn, how well you learn it, and how much it ultimately changes the way you live your life. Accordingly, the Wright educational methodology is driven by the way we teach: we teach in order to support you—and through you, the world—to a conscious, sustainable way of living. This chapter shows how the methodology developed at Wright is based on an educational model in which teaching transforms individuals to live lives of full potential and, through the process, transforms the faculty, the organization, the curriculum, and the world.

The theoretical foundations of the technologies and methods employed at

Wright are actualized through our technology of Wright Performative Education, designed to propel you into creating a great life for yourself. This chapter only covers the most salient aspects of the theories and philosophies that form the foundation of our teaching technology and not the curricular content itself. The thinking of some of the foremost psychologists, philosophers, and systems and learning theorists form the foundation of Wright Performative Education— Vygotsky, Adler, Nietzsche, Kierkegaard, Sartre, Mezirow, and Burns, to name a few. Wright Performative Education has synthesized their theories and given them grounded, practical application to serve a broad range of people in every area of their lives, resulting in transformational education and transformational leadership.

With personal responsibility at its core and choice as the nexus between being and becoming, Wright Performative Education is leadership and learning at its most essential and powerful. As this chapter shows, Wright Performative Education is about discovering, moving beyond that which you already know, becoming something different through your learning, creating a previously unforeseen future—both for you and for the Wright organization—and choosing to step into your next most radiant self. The desire to have our programs accomplish these goals, the wish to have our students be transformed through their learning in order to be, as Vygotsky describes, "both the source and the product of learning" (Holzman, 2000, p.4), propelled the creation of learning technologies that would actively and intentionally allow this to happen.

TOWARD A TECHNOLOGY OF TRANSFORMATIONAL LEARNING

WRIGHT HAS PROVIDED DEVELOPMENTAL AND TRANSFORMATIONAL education successfully to thousands of high-performing adult learners and supported them toward higher levels of personal and professional success in all areas of life: relationships, couples, family, career, leadership, team building, sales, entrepreneurship, life purpose and spirituality, singles, and men's and women's programs. Early in their work at Wright, students tended to not only achieve their initial goals, but also arrive at a high level of sophistication in their awareness of their behaviors and processes. They used this awareness to make dramatic improvements in their lives.

As we worked with our students, as our vision expanded, and as our sense of mission emerged, we found ourselves wanting even more for students in their training. We wanted them to go beyond being great thinkers and achievers to be perpetually evolving to their next, most radiant selves. We wanted them to lead lives of More—excellent lives where quality was maximized in all areas. We wanted them not only to be active participants in their own training, but also to contribute to their fellow students and to the world around them. We wanted them to be profoundly aware of both their current ways of being and of the possibilities of what they themselves could become. We wanted them to hold this vision for those around them, the organizations to which they belonged, and indeed the entire world. We wanted them to have a vision beyond anything they could currently imagine. What we sought was nothing short of global transformation.

We also sought to develop a learning curriculum that would achieve nothing short of a transformation for our students. We designed a curriculum that would give them not just more of what they already had, but more of what really mattered to them, more of what was necessary not only for personal transformation but also for family, organizational, and societal transformation as well.

Our curriculum and teaching technology have evolved and emerged amidst this inquiry and continue to evolve and emerge. We have drawn upon great thinkers from early to contemporary philosophers, educators, and psychologists, to behavioral economists and even futurists and spiritual teachers. As presented in earlier chapters, we drew on Adlerian psychology, existentialist thought, and developmental psychology. We also drew on systems theory and various leadership models. We moved beyond a mere synthesis of these approaches in order to create a sound and dynamic theoretical base for our teaching technologies and methodologies.

We also incorporated learning and developmental theories, most notably those of Lev Vygotsky, in whose performance theories we ground our learning technologies. We have succeeded in taking Vygotsky's performance theories of education beyond their former purely educational settings and stretching their application to lifelong learning, so that they apply to every area of people's lives, creating an entirely new curriculum and method of delivery, which we have named Wright Performative Education.

Our students manifest the potency and effectiveness of the learning technologies of Wright Performative Education in every area of their lives. Many of them have risen to national leadership in arenas such as economics, compensation, and retirement policy. They have achieved positions as executives in public corporations. In our couples program, the divorce rate of those participating for ten years or more is under 4%, compared with the national divorce rate of 50% (Whitehead & Popende, 2006). Our students demonstrate career success that far surpasses national statistics. A survey of 80 of our students resulted in the following conclusions: 7.5% of the student population made $100,000 or more (the national average is 7%) before starting our programs. After participation in our programs, this number increased to 32%. In addition, of those surveyed, 66% reported an increase in income, 54% had been promoted or gotten better jobs, and, of those in sales, 56% reported selling more. In addition, those surveyed reported having more purpose and meaning in their lives, better marriages, deeper friendships, a greater sense of belonging, and greater overall satisfaction in life.

Wright students are transforming their way of being and what they expect from life. They learn to orient to higher principles, as they learn how to operationalize the Wright Model of Personal Growth and Development in their lives. They change not only what they choose to learn but also how they learn and what they can expect from their learning. Wright students are transformed in their new sense of commitment to lifelong learning and development and, as a result, hold their lives as both an adventure and a journey of discovery. They become more open to experiences and more available to receive the abundance that is available to all of us in every area of our life. Wright students become active creators of their experiences, not victims of circumstances.

The Wright curriculum stimulates deep emotional and intellectual learning and provides a way to integrate that learning as long-term change into every area of life. By living these changes, students move into the realm of leadership. As a result, we seek not only to foster individual transformational learning but also to develop transformational leaders who will impact the world around us. As John F. Kennedy once stated, "Leadership and learning are indispensable to each other." We believe that learning to lead a great life leads to leading others, hence our motto: "Lead your life. Lead your world."

THEORETICAL FOUNDATIONS OF WRIGHT PERFORMATIVE EDUCATION

As the needs and the numbers of our student population have grown, so have the complexity of our curriculum and the methods of its delivery. As we learned more and our body of knowledge—both researched and empirical—increased, we found that we were synthesizing and integrating, on an ongoing basis, theories of psychology, philosophy, education, and development. Wright Performative Education evolved from, and is a unique synthesis and application of, this body of theory and philosophy. As presented in previous chapters, our principal foundational theories are those of psychologist Alfred Adler; the existentialist theories propounded by Friedrich Nietzsche, Søren Kierkegaard, Jean-Paul Sartre and others; and the developmental theories of Sigmund Freud and others. The principal foundational educational theories are the performative education theory of psychologist Lev Vygotsky; theories of transformative learning and development; the mistaken beliefs of Alfred Adler; the existential focus on anxiety; systems theories; and transformational leadership theory. The following sections present the theoretical basis of the educational methodologies and learning technologies of Wright Performative Learning and its principal operational technology, the Assignment Way of Living.

THE EDUCATIONAL THEORIES OF LEV VYGOTSKY

Wright Performative Education has its roots in the theories of Lev Vygotsky, who saw human growth as the result of the interaction of people engaging together within their culture, rather than as the external manifestation of an individualized, internal process (Holzman, 2000). Vygotsky believed that we learn through activity and performing, and it is through performing that we learn and develop (Holzman, 2000). However in contradistinction to Piaget, Vygotsky proposed that not only did learning precede development, but it also "pulled and tugged until greater development evolved" (Wink & Putney, 2002, p. 96). According to Vygotsky, in order for this pull to take place, you must do the things that you do not already know how to do, acting as if you already know how to do them. By performing in this way, you step into the unknown and grow, develop, and learn.

Consider young children and their acquisition of language. In the interaction between adult and child, the adult speaks to the child as if the child already knows language. Adults interact with children in a manner that is far beyond what is possible for them considering their current level of development. As a result, children perform beyond what they're capable of doing, and, in that moment, are concurrently performing and becoming themselves. This process of becoming occurs repeatedly throughout human development. Through performance, you evolve and grow from your current states of development to a new, emerging self (Holzman, 2000).

In the acquisition of language, as with any learning process, children encounter that which lies within their immediate level of understanding. This is what Vygotsky termed the Zone of Current Development (ZCD). What children learn within the ZCD is what they can learn on their own, the "actual developmental level as determined by independent problem solving" (Vygotsky, 1978, p. 131).

In order to expand understanding beyond their ZCD, children require modeling and interaction from more knowledgeable others (MKOs), who will introduce them to skills beyond their reach and bring them into what Vygotsky termed the Zone of Proximal Development (ZPD) (Driscoll, 1994). Vygotsky (1978) defines the ZPD as the distance between the "actual developmental level as determined by independent problem solving and the level of potential development as determined through problem solving under adult guidance or in collaboration with more capable peers" (p. 86).

Ultimately Vygotsky's ZCD and ZPD are really states of being and becoming: "each one of us is, at every moment, both being and becoming. The ZPD is the ever emergent and continuously changing 'distance' between being and becoming" (Holzman, 2006, p. 6). As described in Chapters 1 and 2, the concepts of being and becoming are critical to existentialist theory, another basis for Wright Performative Education.

Through performing, children learning language begin to imitate the adult's language and in this process move from their zone of current development to the next level of language in the zone of proximal development. Children develop by performing roles in other areas of their life over and over, and this is a powerful learning mechanism. One result of this repetition is that children perform their way into cultural adaptations and norms. Over time, however, they become routinized and rigid in their behavior. As adults, they then become locked into roles and falsely assume that is who they are.

You may identify yourself, for example, as a specific personality type. You believe that anything other than this identity is not who you are. When challenged with a new way of being, you defend yourself by saying, 'That's not who I am,' or, 'That's not me.' (Holzman, 2000). As you accumulate these declarations of self, they coalesce into sets of beliefs, many of them limiting or even mistaken. The formation of sets or systems of limiting beliefs was the basis of much of Alfred Adler's work, as described in Chapters 1 and 2, and is what the Wright methodology is specifically designed to address.

Followers of Vygotsky developed the concept of performative psychology, which conceives of human life as "primarily performative" and believes that, "we collectively create our lives through performing, simultaneously being who we are and who we are becoming" (Holzman, 2000, p. 1). Performative psychologists believe that your ability to play and improvise is a necessary component of your emotional, social, and intellectual development. Performative psychologists therefore sought to create new environments or stages on which people of all ages could perform, i.e. create their lives.

Vygotsky held the belief that the true essence or purpose of education was to transform not only the student, but the teacher, the curriculum, the school, and the community. Despite its potential for advancing learning and development, performative psychology has been used primarily in therapeutic and educational settings. It has not yet found wider application in people's lives, lifelong learning, and in the world at large. Wright Performative Education uses performance not only in educational settings, but also in every area of people's lives. In the Wright methodology, this is called the Assignment Way of Living.

Wright education holds Vygotsky's concept of transformation being activated by individuals in their own learning as a compelling vision that starts with responsibility, creativity, and courage. To further incorporate those qualities into our way of being as educators, we also draw from other theories about the interaction of transformation and education.

Transformational Learning

In order for us to empower our students to have a life beyond that which they thought possible, a life of More, we realized that we must first create a model of learning beyond that which we thought possible. As a starting point, this model of learning needed to be one that not only resulted in the transformation of its learners, but also incorporated both transmissional learning (where the teacher imparts knowledge) and transactional learning (where students interact with each other and with the faculty) (Miller & Seller, 1990). The most famous proponent of the latter was John Dewey, who developed the theory of experiential education whose tenets prefigured many of the concepts that Vygotsky later developed: the importance of "collateral learning" as a social process rather than one occurring within the individual alone; the action of experience as moving individuals toward and into something new; the transformational possibilities of education; and the precursor of the more knowledgeable other (MKO) as the educator who recognizes which environments "are conducive to having experiences that lead to growth" (Dewey, 1938, p. 40) and who can evaluate the experiences of those having less experience. On the transformational possibilities of experience in education, Dewey stated, "The principle of continuity of experience means that every experience both takes up something from those which have gone before and modifies in some way the quality of those which come after" (Dewey, 1938, p. 35).

On the importance of experience Dewey said, "I assume that amid all uncertainties, there is one permanent frame of reference: namely, the organic connection between education and personal experience; or that the new education is committed to some kind of empirical and experimental philosophy" (Dewey, 1938, p. 25). Experience and experiential learning are the basis for the Wright Assignment Way of Living, the core set of activities that students perform which are woven throughout Wright Performative Education.

As mentioned above, the impetus for our search for a new model of learning and the belief that such a model was possible came from both our experience in serving our students over the years and from a profound consideration of the work of previous noteworthy thinkers on theories of learning. The notion of a type of learning that both transcends the acquisition of knowledge and also fundamentally changes the person who is learning was described by Jack Mezirow, who developed a theory of deep learning beyond information acquisition. Mezirow termed this type of education "transformative learning," which is moving beyond the acquisition of factual knowledge alone to instead becoming changed by what you learn in some meaningful way (Boyd, 1988). This process, he says, includes a "perspective transformation" (Mezirow, 1997). The notion of perspective transformation is developed by Edmund O'Sullivan (2002), who provides a powerful description of transformative learning:

> Transformative learning involves experiencing a deep, structural shift in the basic premises of thought, feelings, and actions. It is a shift of consciousness that dramatically and irreversibly alters our way of being in the world. Such a shift involves our understanding of ourselves and our self-locations; our relationships with other humans and with the natural world; ... our visions of alternative approaches to living" (p.18).

Social psychologist and humanistic philosopher Erich Fromm (1981) describes this transformation in his discussion of the "having" and "being" mode of existence:

> Students in the having mode of existence will listen to a lecture, hearing the words and understanding their logical structure and their meaning and, as best they can, will write down every word in their notebooks—so that, later on, they can memorize their notes and thus pass an exam-

ination. But the content does not become part of their own individual system of thought, enriching and widening it. (pp. 17-18)

Contrast this with his description of the "being mode":

...listen, they hear, and most important, they receive and they respond in an active, productive way. What they listen to stimulates their own thinking processes. New questions, new ideas, new perspectives arise in their minds. Their listening is an alive process . . . They do not simply acquire knowledge that they can take home and memorize. Each student has been affected and has changed: each is different after the lecture than he or she was before it. (p. 18)

Fromm is not merely describing a difference in learning styles, but rather a deeper, essential change.

Carl Rogers (1962), a founder of the humanistic approach to psychology, describes a similar experience in his definition of significant learning:

By significant learning, I mean learning which is more than an accumulation of facts. It is learning which makes a difference in the individual's behavior, in the course of action he chooses in the future, in his attitudes and in his personality. It is a pervasive learning which is not just an accretion of knowledge, but which interpenetrates with every portion of his existence. (p. 280)

Wright education seeks to encompass Rogers' thinking by helping students apply these concepts with two distinctions:

1. learning, which is knowing or understanding something that they did not know before.
2. growing, which means doing something that they have not done before.

Both learning and growing are necessary for transformational learning, for it is through the process of learning and growing that you move from being to becoming. Development is not an achieved state, but something that must be continuously created through ongoing choice, as the existential philosophers described.

Given the centrality of choice in existentialist thought, you can begin to see the existentialist implications for learning and development.

Transformation allows the student to lead a better life, but how is this transformation initiated and facilitated? In our teaching experience at Wright, we knew that life-changing events sometimes resulted in sudden epiphanies or a change in attitude that altered the course of a student's life. We wondered how we could create the conditions that would enable transformation to happen in students' lives, not just once and not passively through external circumstances, but actively and on an ongoing basis.

A clue to this query lies in the work of Jerome Bruner (1971), who believed that in order to create the experience of significant learning, you must depart from the rote acceptance of pre-conceived notions and received wisdom and engage in an active process of discovery:

> The hypothesis I would propose here is to the degree that one is able to approach learning as a task of discovering something rather than "learning about" it, to that degree there will be a tendency . . . to work with the autonomy of self-reward or, more properly, be rewarded by discovery itself. (pp. 87-88)

If discovery is the key to significant learning, then why not create a system in which discovery is an ongoing activity? The system developed at Wright, one that actually is the product of a long evolution in our support of students, is called the Assignment Way of Living. The Assignment Way of Living is the explicit and ongoing experiential activity of engaging in new behaviors and performing new roles thereby challenging limiting beliefs, disrupting routinized ways of being, upsetting automatic systems, teaching new life skills, and launching us into a journey of personal discovery.

ADLERIAN PSYCHOLOGY: MISTAKEN BELIEFS AND BEHAVIOR

Achieving the type of perspective transformation described by Mezirow of necessity requires us to make a systematic accounting of our currently held beliefs and how they affect our lives. Alfred Adler, the Austrian psychiatrist who was one of Freud's most notable students, did extensive work on the function of our beliefs in defining who we are. Adler departed from traditional psychoanalysis and focused on man as a social being. Like Vygotsky, he saw man in a socio-cultural context. As initially presented in Chapter 2, Adler believed that your behaviors and choices are largely shaped by the unconscious beliefs that you learned about the world in your earliest life experiences as a child, and that it was those beliefs, both accurate and inaccurate, that were the lens through which you create your experience. Adler postulated that it is your beliefs that shape what you can expect from the world and what the world expects of you, what is allowed and what is not allowed. These beliefs, learned in childhood, are what you, often unconsciously, continue to believe today. Adler (1927) felt that by uncovering these beliefs and learning and practicing new behaviors, adults could shift long-standing behavioral patterns and begin to act contrary to ways that would be indicated by their unconscious beliefs.

In the Adlerian framework that serves as the basis of the Wright model and is incorporated into Wright education, it is the constellation of mistaken beliefs that determines your behaviors in life. You will tend to act in ways that reaffirm those beliefs. This is commonly referred to as a self-fulfilling prophecy, which serves to further justify and entrench your beliefs. In the grips of a self-fulfilling prophecy, even when you see evidence to the contrary, you frequently ignore it or excuse it as a fluke or accident, choosing to operate in ways that affirm your preexisting beliefs rather than shifting to new beliefs.

As noted in Chapter 2, American psychologist and educator Rudolph Dreikurs brought Adlerian theory to the United States. He referred to the matrix of your beliefs as the lifestyle (Beames, 1984), the summary of your beliefs and ways of being. Dreikurs said that you can learn to shift the limiting elements of your lifestyle and maximize your potential by identifying basic mistakes, self-defeating "self-talk," or limiting beliefs. By challenging these limiting beliefs, you can operate in new ways and implement new behaviors formerly prohibited by your old beliefs (Schulman & Dreikurs, 1978). Dreikurs' description of the lifestyle as an amalgam of beliefs and behaviors approaches the Wright education understanding of what constitutes a system.

It is in Wright learning labs in particular, as described below, that the Wright education methodology relates Mezirow's transformative learning theory and his concept of perspective transformation to Adler's work on mistaken beliefs. Perspective transformation is defined by Mezirow as "the process of becoming critically aware of how and why our assumptions have come to constrain the way we perceive, understand, and feel about our world." (Mezirow, 1991, p. 167). Mezirow says that transformative learning happens as individuals change their frames of reference by using autonomous or critical thinking—reflecting on their assumptions and beliefs and consciously making and implementing plans that result in new ways of defining their worlds (Mezirow, 1997). The learning labs at Wright operationalize those concepts in a way that introduces a profound existential component to this transformative foundation.

EXISTENTIALISM: EXISTENTIAL ANXIETY AND THE CHOICE OF BECOMING

Existential philosophy emerged during the 1800s as a new ideology and commitment to being alive in the world and experiencing life with passion and awareness. Its earliest proponents were Kierkegaard and Nietzsche, and it had as its main themes the concepts of freedom, choice, responsibility, and courage. With its central proposition "existence precedes essence," existentialism makes a distinction between the way you have been and how you are becoming. In the former, unconscious patterns of behaviors that are comfortable and based on past mistaken beliefs limit your potential. In order to achieve your potential, it is necessary to engage in new behaviors that operate outside the prescribed patterns of what is comfortable. Nietzsche (1889) believed that in order to do this you must recover your aliveness and vitality, leaving behind hypocritical, moral limitations. The principle of choice—that you are responsible for creating who you are—is one of Kierkegaard's (1843) most important contributions to psychological theory and also has implications for developmental theory.

Choice is the sine qua non of existentialist thought. It is the pivot between your being and what you are becoming. Consciousness of the choices available creates anxiety, another key existential concept. There is constant choice between the comfortable 'old' way of being and taking a risk to do things differently, with unknown consequences. At any given moment you have a choice to move from your conception of yourself and your beliefs to choose new behaviors that teach you new skills, to achieve greater self-awareness, and realize new possibilities of what you can be. There is a sense of upset that all humans share when they contemplate these possibilities and the freedom to choose them. Kierkegaard (1980) describes this feeling of upset as "existential anxiety". "Anxiety is, therefore, the spirit's awareness of the possibility of knowledge and the possibility of being able to be something other than what it is. Briefly put, anxiety is awareness of our freedom to know and to be able (p. 2)."

The choice of becoming, the choice to move into the unknown, is what leads you to your emerging self. On the other hand, when you choose to do what is comfortable—when you hold back your desires out of fear or discomfort—rather than what you sense is right or challenging, you experience a phenomenon that existentialists have named "ontological guilt" (Firestone, 1987). Ontological guilt is the inner sense that comes from knowing that you did not choose to become what you could have become. The denial that you had a choice at all was named by Sartre; he called this denial "bad faith" (Sartre, 1956).

> The issue of bad faith for Sartre is one of denying this freedom [of choice] and this responsibility [to choose]. To be fully responsible for ourselves is a source of great anxiety. Most of us don't want to experience that anxiety, so we look outside ourselves to provide justifications for our actions. We look to the other to define us: to prevailing social roles and expectations, to accepted family patterns, to what others want us to be (Wright & Medlock, 1994, p. 15).

You are in bad faith and lead an inauthentic life when you choose to act as if your rationalizations, the reasons you make up for why you do or do not do something, are real and valid. When you deny that you have the opportunity to make a different choice and do something different, and when you don't accept your choices as your own, you are acting in bad faith.

At the same time, ontological guilt is a powerful force. The denial and suppression of it in your life manifests itself in many forms. Notable among these are so-called "lifestyle" choices, the habits you might develop to numb or distract yourself from the discomfort of your bad faith and your ontological guilt, such as overusing television, shopping, food, and sex. The term Dr. Judith Wright coined for these habits and routines is "soft addictions," which can lead to blocks in students' development, and Wright has developed an entire curriculum to address this significant phenomenon (Wright, 2003, 2006).

Existentialist thought, particularly the notion of choice, informs Wright Performative Education very powerfully. It is through choosing what you can become, rather than practicing what you already know, that you responsibly step into the unknown and create authorship in your life, in keeping with Level Five of the Wright model.

Systems Theory

Though not systems theorists, both Adler and Vygotsky saw individuals acting, learning, and developing in the context of a larger whole. This type of understanding, as well as an understanding of systems theory, are integral to Wright Performative Education.

A system is any set of entities that operate in collaboration and that produce some result. A system can be anything from a single organism or individual to an organization or a society. Systems theory and systems thinking have emerged and evolved from being a method of research and understanding to being a tool of intervention, planning, and design.

Traditional science began to study complex systems by reducing a system to its parts and studying how those parts interacted with each other. Though this approach became widely used and successful in physical sciences such as biology, chemistry, and physics, it led to reductionist thinking and therefore became limiting (Fuller, 1981). Reducing a system to a set of objects loses sight of the importance of the environment in which the system and its components exist. Systems thinker Ludwig von Bertalanffy (1969) addressed the importance of the environment in his General System Theory.

The psychiatrist Dr. Murray Bowen extended the scope of systems theory with his Family Systems Theory (1985), which is used extensively in the Wright methodology. The systemic approach to family dynamics and issues introduced by Bowen helped to de-pathologize individuals, the so-called "problem child," and see how individuals were more the manifestation of issues occurring over the entire family system. Bowen proposed that individuals cannot be understood in isolation from one another, but rather as a part of a larger system that seeks to keep all the family members in the same roles and patterns of communication and dialogue.

Critical to systems theory is the notion that systems work to maintain homeostasis, self-regulation, and control, concepts brought to light by Walter Cannon in 1932. Systems have internal relationships among constituent objects, and when upset is created, the system seeks to maintain itself and bring itself back into balance. For this reason system change is difficult to sustain and presents significant challenges to transformational education, which is strongly addressed in the Wright methodology.

In Dr. Judith Wright's early research with children with developmental disabilities and their families at the University of Illinois and the Illinois Department of Developmental Disabilities, she developed model programs that reflected a systems approach, which received several major national research and demonstration grants. Dr. Wright and her staff realized that working solely with the child, outside of the family and environment, was insufficient to effect the changes sought. Incorporating Sameroff and Chandler's transactional model of child development (1975), Dr. Wright and her staff focused on the interactions and transactions among children, their parents, and the environment and each element's influence on the other and the system. They developed programs that worked with the family, the child, and to some degree, their environment in an integrated way. Their research proved the significant effectiveness of this approach over programs that only intervened with the child. (Wright, 1982)

In that early research, Dr. Wright developed and designed transdisciplinary treatment where all providers (physical therapists, educators, social workers, occupational therapists, etc.) focused on the whole child. Through learning each others' disciplines, they developed a systems approach to the whole child, not just the "parts" they were trained to observe and intervene in by their discipline. In addition, they taught the parents to "work" with their children in natural ways, integrating therapeutic interventions in the course of normal play, daily life, and interactions (Wright, 1982). They also further expanded their programs to teach and support parents and professionals to work as partners, resulting in a comprehensive synergy to best serve the child, the family, the service providers, the institution, and the schools (Wright, 1984). The success of these holistic programs served as an inspiration for and precursor to the comprehensive systems approach at Wright.

TRANSFORMATIONAL LEADERSHIP THEORY

Existential philosophy is concerned with the notions of being and becoming and personal responsibility. Systems theory seeks to identify the ways that entities interact and influence each other. Both hold significance to the topic of transformational leadership.

Although there have been many theories of leadership, and many continue to develop, Wright focuses on a theory of leadership first introduced by James MacGregor Burns called transformational leadership, in part because many of Burns' themes resonate with Vygotsky's teachings on transformation. For instance, Burns' description of the relationship between leadership and personal development is particularly relevant to the training curriculum at Wright:

> Transforming leadership. . . occurs when one or more persons engage with others in such a way that leaders and followers raise one another to higher levels of motivation and morality. Their purposes, which might have started out as separate but related, as in the case of transactional leadership, become fused. Transforming leadership ultimately...raises the level of human conduct and ethical aspiration of both leader and led, and thus it has a transforming effect on both (Burns, 1978, p. 20).

Burns describes the potential of transformational leadership to transform the organizations where such leadership is practiced by raising both the standards and the levels of conduct of its members and its leaders. This change—and here, note echoes of Vygotsky's thinking—is effected not just by the action of individuals but by mutual engagement and collaboration, which are what transforms the organization. Organizational change and management expert Robert Quinn (1996) later continued the association between leadership training and transformational education: "One key to successful leadership is continuous personal change. Personal change is a reflection of our inner growth and empowerment" (p. 166).

Management and organizational change expert Peter Senge relates transformational leadership to transformational education in his work on learning organizations. Senge describes learning organizations as:

> . . .organizations where people continually expand their capacity to create the results they truly desire, where new and expansive patterns of thinking are nurtured, where collective aspiration is set free, and where people are continually learning to see the whole together (Senge, 1990, p. 3).

Senge also points to the larger possibilities that learning organizations hold for the world: "The commitment required to build learning organizations goes beyond people's typical 'commitment to their organizations.' It encompasses commitment to changes needed in the larger world and to seeing our organizations as vehicles for bringing about such changes" (Senge, 1994, p. 17).

The notion of an organization that is not merely an entity which has the potential to change the world, but that has as its commitment the mission to bring about such change holds particular significance for Wright, where leadership of your life and of the world set the context for all we do.

THE WRIGHT MODEL OF PERFORMATIVE EDUCATION: INTEGRATING THEORY INTO PRACTICE

Wright Performative Education puts into real-world practice a synthesis of technologies previously understood intellectually and of limited application, but yet undelivered in the comprehensive, proven, and life-changing way that has produced such impressive results for Wright students.

Wright Performative Education is a method of delivery that synthesizes the theories and thinking of the foremost philosophers, psychologists, and cutting-edge systems, learning, and educational theorists. The synthesis of the foundational theories of Wright Performative Education creates an exciting and hitherto unseen level of synergy by drawing on the revolutionary educational theories of Vygotsky on performance and learning; by living his constant process of both being and becoming through performing that which one does not yet know how to do; by expanding the vision of possibilities and development through more knowledgeable others; and by fulfilling Vygotsky's vision of transformational education that transforms the students, MKOs, faculty, coaches, the curriculum, Wright, and the greater world.

The synergy builds from bringing existential theory into living reality through stepping into the unknown; by altering ways of being through Mezirow's transformational learning and perspective transformation; by being in Bruner's process of discovery; by experiencing Fromm's "being mode"; by engaging in Rogers' concept of significant learning; by breaking out of Adler's constellation of mistaken and limiting beliefs; by realizing Burns' transformational leadership theory; and by transforming our systems to transform our way of being, our lives, and the world around us.

Wright Performative Education trains students, from beginners to advanced, to recognize their innate leadership and their potential to create their lives. Our programs allow participants to create opportunities for learning through growth activities and events, life assignments, mentoring and support of students as more knowledgeable others (MKOs), and participation in and leadership roles on designated projects. Through these events, in addition to learning new skills, our students are able to assess their current influence on the world; uncover unconscious, limited, or hidden beliefs; and understand the larger workings of the systems of which they are a part. Wright students use what they have learned to make desired changes in behavior, choose other beliefs, and thereby intervene in both their internal and external systems. They subsequently achieve desired outcomes consciously and with increasing effectiveness, all the while stepping into ever newer and more advanced levels of leadership, personal development, and creation.

As students engage in this process, they themselves are not only transforming, but also the leaders and educators are transforming. What is more, the curriculum itself is constantly transforming to the point that, as an institution, Wright continually witnesses the emergence of the next evolution of its curriculum and teaching technology. Wright has, in essence, set up a game of constant evolution that challenges everyone, including the organization itself, to constantly stretch into their unknown potential, a process Wright leaders describe to students as the "emergence of your next most radiant self."

Wright students engage fully in the process of transformation because they daily expand their capacity to learn and grow. Accordingly, Wright has rigorously applied Vygotsky's concept of an ever-expanding field of development, continually being stretched by the performative learning activities that precede development in the form of assignments.

Neither linear nor incremental, Vygotsky's transformational development was envisioned by James Zebroski as a tidal wave. He proposed this concept of development in contradistinction to either Step or Stage Theories, which highlight the incremental or discrete stages of development:

> In this metaphor, development is both progressive and regressive. However when the movement is progressive, the wave becomes deeper and higher as it moves forward, exemplifying the cumulative effect of increased development. By looking at the tidal wave, we see that past experiences continually transform themselves as the foundation for the next wave of development (Wink & Putney, 2002, p. 89).

The experience with students at Wright shows that theoretical knowledge and personal data alone, including insights and skills acquired through transmissional learning, are not sufficient to bring about lasting changes in your life. Moreover, the Wright experience shows that you must account for the regressive phases of development. The amount of continual, external support you need in effecting changes in systems should not be underestimated. As Vygotsky stated, growth and development must necessarily be part of an "ongoing creative and collaborative" process. With that in mind, the MKO is integrated into all aspects of the Wright Performative Education curriculum as students move from their ZCD to their ZPD.

Through coaching, teaching, intervening, and providing feedback, MKOs (whether faculty, staff, or more advanced students) model possibilities. They provide support and accountability to maintain changes already made and further challenge, support, and encourage students by raising the bar of expectation and holding a higher vision for them. They teach skills, challenge belief systems, and create an environment for the student's next most radiant self to emerge. MKOs also introduce students to the theoretical and methodological foundations of what they are experiencing while they are experiencing it. In an unusual approach to service delivery at Wright called "mutuality", everyone—students, teachers, coaches, lab leaders, trainers, and staff—engages in the process of learning, growing, and transforming, all with different roles at times, but transparent to each other.

Following Senge's thinking, Wright is a learning organization focused on transformational learning and leadership. Students and staff are invested in each other's growth and development, holding vision for each other, while providing support, mentoring, modeling, feedback, skill development, and mutual facilitation. Wright fosters a growth-oriented culture where students have repeated contact with certain MKOs and cyclical contact with others, developing ongoing relationships of mutual empowerment. Students consistently apply the skills they are learning in relationship with each other while at the same time learning new skills. As students progress, they move from being learning participants in training activities to serving participants who themselves are also learning, and, wherever possible, becoming deliverers of coaching and training as well as facilitators of learning laboratories.

THE TECHNOLOGY OF
WRIGHT PERFORMATIVE EDUCATION

The synergy of developmental, systems, existential, learning, and leadership philosophies and theories is crystallized in the learning technology of Wright Performative Education. Our teaching technology is woven throughout all of our programs and coursework in all areas of life including personal transformation, relationships, career, sales, entrepreneurship, singles, men's, women's, gay studies, spirituality and life purpose, teamwork, communication, leadership, and more. Wright's three key modalities of delivery—seminars and trainings, learning labs, and individual coaching—combine transmissional, transactional, and transformational learning. Woven throughout the entire structure is the Assignment Way of Living. The Assignment Way of Living, referenced earlier, and the three modalities combine to create the technology of Wright Performative Education, and a unique transformational learning and leadership community.

Although any one modality alone—seminar, learning lab, or coaching—is certainly helpful, Wright has learned over time that it is the synergy of the three modalities that results in the profound student successes cited in the beginning of this chapter. When students participate in only one or two components (meet with an individual coach, attend a training seminar, or participate in a lab) they have positive results, but they do not approach the results of those who participate in all three modalities combined. The synergy of the three modalities provides the support the student needs—in the form of MKOs—to expand their zone of proximal development, and opportunities for perspective transformation, transformational learning, and transformational leadership.

In addition to the three modalities, Wright Performative Education builds accountability into the process. Students create visions, set goals, and engage in periodic reviews. The following sections explain the modalities and accountabilities of Wright Performative Education.

Seminars and Trainings

Wright seminars and trainings, whether conducted over a week, a weekend, a day, or an evening, provide experiential and didactic education where students learn the theoretical foundations of what they are experiencing while experiencing the theories and content they are learning. Seminars and trainings not only set context and define the higher purpose for all other Wright Performative Education activities but also provide an experiential base and focus for continued learning. Seminars and trainings are designed to assist students to think things that they have never thought before and do things that they have not done before—to experience choice and step into the unknown, to face their existential anxiety and step into new possibilities. Evening seminars provide some experiential components in addition to didactic elements, but these are not as extensively employed as in longer trainings.

Longer trainings, particularly weekend or week-long trainings, immerse students in different ways of thinking, being, and living—providing opportunities for them to experience Mezirow's perspective transformation through experiential activities, exercises, working with MKOs, and being exposed to new thinking and viewpoints. Students participate in active exercises to learn and practice new skills, stretching into new possibilities. They are often given overnight assignments where they are challenged to perform in their lives in new and different ways that help them to learn and practice new skills. Assignments are designed not only to build new skills reflecting the performance learning of Vygotsky, but also to help the student impact their constellation of mistaken beliefs as identified by Adler.

Students expand their Zone of Proximal Development as defined by Vygotsky through interaction with more knowledgeable others and report significant growth from these trainings. The exercises performed in seminars and trainings are the on-ramp to the more extensive performance of assignments that takes place in other components of Wright Performative Education. Seminars can be on a variety of subjects from career to sales, parenting, and singlehood. Key trainings focus on the Wright Model of Personal Growth and Development as a way to put it into action in students' lives. Those trainings include Vision in Action (Adler's spheres expanded), Applied Early Childhood Development, Applied Adolescent and Adult Development, Living a Principled Life, and the Year of More. The impact of the seminars and trainings is solidified and multiplied by the student's participation in the other learning modalities—learning labs and coaching.

Vision

Vision is a component of all Wright activities. Students develop and orient to vision in most trainings and seminars. Vision is formally taught and facilitated in the Vision in Action Seminar and updated three times a year in growth and progress reviews. In that training, each individual develops a vision statement in each of the seven areas of life in the Wright model. These statements are then ideally used as guiding lights and touchstones during their work during their learning labs and coaching throughout the trimester

Learning Laboratories

Learning labs are a special part of Wright Performative Education. Learning labs typically consist of eight to twelve members, peers who function as MKOs for each other, as well as a leader or facilitator who is also participating in his or her own transformational learning. Within the lab, participants apply the theory and skills they have already learned in seminars. They learn new skills and challenge limiting beliefs with the support, mentoring, and coaching of other lab members and the leader. Labs are offered in all curricular areas such as personal transformation, sales, career, couples, singles, family, lifestyles, men's, women's, leadership, and spirituality.

In a learning lab, the members, who are often at different stages of development in their growth, interact with one another in an experiential l learning environment. Lab leaders and lab members with more experience in certain areas become the MKOs for less experienced members. Every member of the lab has an assignment specific to an area of their own personal growth that they perform in the lab as well as in their everyday life. This assignment serves as their newly targeted ZPD. In addition to lab leaders, other members of the group who might have completed a specific assignment can serve as the MKOs to support and encourage those who are new to these assignments. This is consistent with the Wright approach of mutuality, in which everyone is learning and growing all the time as well as fostering the learning and development of others.

At the end of each assignment period, students reflect and report on what they have learned and how they have grown. Growing is demonstrated by doing something they wouldn't have done before. Learning is knowing or understanding something they didn't know before. The students do not fully complete the assignment until they teach what they have learned to someone else, coaching them toward a new behavior. This aspect of completing assignments comes from our firm belief and experience that we need to teach what we learn to solidly integrate it into our lives.

On one level participants learn vicariously by watching someone senior to them, but the potency and effectiveness of Wright Performative Education in the learning lab setting goes even deeper. Learning labs are a venue where students experience an expanded range of possibilities provided by shifts in their own behavior and that of other group members. This environment of experimentation and learning fundamentally upsets the student's comfortable, familiar, and routinely performed systems of behaviors and expectations and forces the student to confront, on an existential level, who they are and who they could become, the workings of their own systems, and the choices available to them to confront their concept of reality.

This consciously disruptive environment fits Mezirow's description of transformative education, which could easily describe the existential experience of our learning labs:

> An experience that cannot be accepted within the confines of that established worldview, but which is compelling is, in the terms of transformative learning, a disorienting dilemma. This dilemma leads to reflection, or a re-evaluation of the previously accepted worldview. Thus the disorienting dilemma provides a new perspective of the

world and a change, or a transformation, of the accepted definition of the world (Merriam & Caffarella, 1991, p. 14).

In Wright learning students begin "the process of ...changing these structures of habitual expectation to make possible a more inclusive, discriminating, and integrating perspective; and finally, making choices or otherwise acting upon these new understandings" (Mezirow, 1991, p. 167). In this learning milieu the peer group is a metaphor for the world and an extreme practice field for one's life. It is a microcosmic practice ground where students can engage in behaviors that would be unacceptable in everyday life, thereby expanding their capacities and expectations and range of acceptable activities at an extraordinary level in every-day life.

Students learn and practice a range of skills, depending on the subject area. They perform these assignments in their daily life and report to the lab on their progress, challenges, and results. They strategize how to be successful, hold each other accountable, and give and receive support. Lab members "check in" midway to their next scheduled meeting on what they are learning and how they are grow-ing related to their life assignments. They report on what mistaken beliefs are being challenged and any blocks they have encountered. This check-in serves as a point of consciousness to either do more of what is working, or to shift, realign, or redouble their efforts in the assignment before the next lab.

It is rare in personal development to have so many people invested in each other's success who also know and support each other over a period of time. Lab mates are aware of each other's patterns, share a deep knowledge of each other, and serve as leaders to one another. Learning labs are a powerful force in trans-formational learning where the students, the leader, the curriculum, and the lab are in a state of continual transformation.

Coaching

Coaching is a process of personal interaction with another individual in order to foster effectiveness, performance, personal development, and growth. At Wright, effective coaching involves coaches who are themselves active participants in their own transformational learning. These coaches support students to develop new skills, establish goals and visions, and develop a game plan for achieving those goals. They provide focus, direction, encouragement, and feedback. They help stu-dents see and appreciate their strengths as well as understand and overcome their weaknesses. Individual coaching helps students both to maintain system changes and to identify new system changes. For example, someone might attend a weekend seminar and learn new lessons about himself, have several "a-ha" moments, but return to old patterns several days after the weekend training ends. As soon as one returns to one's environment and old ways of being, the system seeks to return to "normal." In one-on-one sessions, the coach, as MKO, helps the student to process the knowledge and skills obtained in the experiences in learning labs, seminars and trainings to leverage these experiences going forward in subsequent lab sessions and, more importantly, into all areas of their lives.

Coaching is generally a one-on-one encounter between the coach and the student or client. Most Wright coaching begins with an assessment of motivation, present circumstances, review of attempts to accomplish goals in the past, establishment of an agreed upon vision and, finally, articulation of goals and methods to fulfill that vision. This is vision coaching. The coaches also hold a vision for their students that is beyond what the students envision for themselves in their zone of current development. By expecting growth from students and by treating them as if they are capable of living into the vision, coaches propel their students beyond what they previously believed they could accomplish and into their new zone of development. Vision coaching helps students identify their visions and goals in all areas of life. Students set weekly goals, with accountability and rewards built in to support goal achievement.

MORE Intimacy Training, another form of coaching at Wright, works at three levels of relationship: 1) your relationship with yourself; 2) your relationship with your more intimacy trainer (coach), which involves a one-to-one, in-the-moment, spontaneous engagement with another human being developed through trust, in order to transform your primary relationship skills; and 3) your relationship with the world. Wright coaches and lifelong learners learn to identify assumptions, beliefs, early experiences and unmet ego development needs in such a way that you can make developmentally supportive choices using actions that may previously have been outside your repertoire of conditioned responses—a second order change of both a gradual and cataclysmic nature.

Goals

Goals are generally set in the context of a larger vision that articulates the intent of the goal. Visions are initially set upon beginning coaching, participating in a seminar, or training. Goals are also set upon joining a transformations or other learning laboratory. At Wright, goals are reviewed on a trimesterly basis. Each goal is accompanied by assignments that will help the individual focus on developing new behaviors that help them accomplish the goal. Goals are concrete and measurable and are achieved or discarded over time as the lifelong learner deepens his/her vision for his/her life. Goals are intended as specific milestones to support behavior modification for the purpose of moving toward the lifelong learner's vision. Goals are adjusted as the student develops. An early goal might be to increase one's fulfillment in friendship by sharing more deeply, and later goals might be to have more supportive, highly motivated friends.

The Assignment Way of Living

The Assignment Way of Living is woven throughout all three modalities of seminars, coaching, and learning labs. This is a ground breaking technology that constitutes the essential pivot point between theory and its real-life application. This unique process provides an integrative, proven ladder of life-altering assignments—each designed to correct core mistaken beliefs, build a new skill, and provide the cumulative building blocks to effect phenomenal life transformation. Through Wright Performative Education and the Assignment Way of Living, students have the opportunity to challenge firmly held beliefs, to continually learn and apply new life skills, to learn about the power of their choices, to see themselves as part of a greater whole and as having influence on those around them, to become—in a striking, powerful, and immediate way—the person they always knew they were meant to be.

Students perform life assignments, doing that which they do not know how to do, performing their way into their next most radiant selves. Rather than practicing what they have always done, students are trained to constantly step into the unknown, face their existential anxiety, avoid building ontological guilt, and be in a continual process of both being and becoming. Through performing assignments, they learn, grow, and develop, becoming more than they were before, actualizing Vygotsky's learning theory. Assignments provide a continual process of discovery as described by Bruner.

Students receive daily, weekly, or monthly assignments to perform both in their learning labs and in their life. Assignments are far from a random collection of exercises and advice; they are used to focus the student's growth. Each assignment has four aims 1) to challenge a mistaken belief as discussed in Adlerian approaches; 2) to release energy bound by that belief; 3) to redirect that energy; and 4) to experiment with new behaviors and direct the unblocked energy into new behaviors or skills. Assignments are based on the Wright Model of Personal Growth and Development, described in Chapter 3, which unfolds step by step to build a cohesive platform for maximized lifelong learning. This model is grounded in an understanding of how human beings naturally learn and grow, developing skills in both being and doing.

In addition to this sequenced, codified array of assignments, students may take on ad hoc assignments tailored to a specific area or particular issue. Assignments take students into areas they would otherwise avoid. The Assignment Way of Living provides direction toward desired outcomes. Engaging in the assignments raises awareness, builds skills, expands the range of emotional expression, increases communication ability, and builds students' behavioral repertoire to transform their lives. Through the Assignment Way of Living, students learn to approach the rest of their lives as a perpetual adventure, a continuous journey of learning and growing.

Assignments, generated and performed on a continuing basis, operate to facilitate human development in context by challenging the core beliefs, which, as taught by Adler, serve to maintain systems. The performance of assignments challenges core beliefs, generates new behaviors, and disrupts systems, thereby facilitating personal transformation and development. This can best be done in a context where your internal system and the external system that maintains that internal system can simultaneously be challenged. Those who attempt to generate new behaviors without challenging their external systems generally fail to maximize their potential. On the other hand, by shifting old patterns, you bring to consciousness a wealth of talents, skills, and ways of being and acting that were hitherto unavailable.

Assignments compel you to question the repetitive performance of old roles and drive you to dig deeply into the rules, myths, and beliefs that govern your behavior and order your systems. These systems of rules, myths, and beliefs operate in all areas of life. One such mistaken belief could be "I am unlovable." There is generally a good deal of pain accompanying the realization of this belief. The pain is often released along with anger, fear, and other emotions that are part of the energy that was blocked with this belief. The released emotion leads to new behaviors that were previously unacceptable and the new behaviors are practiced with the assignment, thereby developing new skills. The goal is to learn to live from a new, more productive belief such as, "I am lovable." Along with this, the assignment helps the learner develop new behaviors in consonance with the new belief such as increased communication, assertiveness, or teamwork, to make progress toward the student's vision. In this case, to be lovable may mean expressing more emotions, risking in relationships, expressing criticisms and needs, or displaying a host of other new behaviors.

Assignments are generally given or reviewed on a weekly basis and flow from the visions and goals a student has identified. Assignments are also designed for each level of the Wright model. Depending on the identified problem area we will determine which assignment is given. For example, one of the Wright life assignments is "asking for things." In this assignment, you ask for as many things as possible in as many situations as possible in your life. You may find that you have difficulty asking for things, whether the request is big, like asking for help moving, or small, like borrowing a book. You may realize that you have been living by rules that limit what you may ask for, whom you may ask for things from, or how much you may ask for.

By engaging in the assignment, you confront the rules you live by, what you believe may happen (beliefs) if you broke any of these rules, and what events or stories (myths) occurred earlier in your life on which you based your rules and beliefs. The assignment allows you to experience your own and others' reactions to your requests, challenge your existing beliefs, make different choices about your behavior, and experience different outcomes. After doing the "asking for things" assignment, many students report how shocked they are at how much people want to help them and how much others are willing to give them. They start to shift their beliefs of scarcity and the beliefs that prevent them from asking for things in life. As a result, they build their sense of entitlement and deserving. They begin to ask for more out of life—and get it.

Considered by themselves, these results alone would come close to achieving Carl Rogers' description of "significant learning." Yet, as that example shows, what makes learning through Wright Performative Education truly significant is the fact that Wright students are both a part of the change process and its agent. Students increasingly generate their own learning and discovery. They become the vehicle of their own transformation. At Wright, we incorporate into performative education what Holzman describes as "the unity of process and product," Vygotsky's dialectical relationship between learning and development, "inseparably intertwined and emergent" (Holzman, in press).

That is the essence of leadership and empowerment—both individually and for others. The empowerment of students is manifested in the way that the external Assignment Way of Living they practice becomes internalized as the assignment way of life. The exterior guidance of the more knowledgeable others transforms into a system of interior guidance whereby students take on assignments and live them without being aware of consciously doing so. The process of being and becoming is now a constant one of ongoing transformation. Students at Wright experience "consciously leading" their lives and discover this also has a powerful influence on others.

Reviews

Student reviews at Wright generally occur three times a year and allow the student to review their progress on their goals and visions. Students in labs receive feedback from other lab members, lab leaders, and their coaches. They identify their next area of work and development for the upcoming trimester. In reviews, goals are updated, assignments completed are addressed, learns and grows are discussed, and new directions are set. Students generally review their assignments daily and monthly, writing a summary of learns and grows. Some of the labs give grades on assignments. The grading is generally an iterative process of the student self-grading, followed by the lab grading, and concluded with a synthesis led by the facilitator if the students did not arrive at consensus.

Leadership

The creation and holding of a leadership context and the assumption that we are all leading all the time inform every phase of Wright Performative Education. The watchwords: "Lead your life. Lead your world" are the central theme of all of the work at Wright. As all students, whether new or long-standing, engage in the activity of their individual transformational education, they automatically become distinguished as leaders, or at the very least, highly engaged and effective team members in whatever setting they happen to be. As engaged team members, our students positively impact others. This occurs not only in the learning lab or group in which they happen to be a participant, but also in ever-widening contexts and settings—whether it be a chance meeting in the hall, an ad hoc gathering or meeting, or a seminar with hundreds of people. The culture of leadership at Wright informs every interaction. Wright creates an environment where an increasing sense of commitment and authorship of success in one's own life results in a commitment to, and responsibility for, everyone else's success. We have therefore come to expect that what the individual learns in the achievement of a great life for himself will inevitably result in his contributing to the great lives of others.

We have provided intensive leadership training for many years (including training in group process, principled leadership, and feminine leadership models, to name a few) for those students who had leadership roles in their businesses, organizations, and corporations. Yet we began to see that these students (who had clearly defined leadership roles) were not the only ones who were positively influencing the lives of those around them. As our other students were transforming their own lives, they were also transforming their relationships, families, businesses, communities, and, in some cases, having an impact at national policy levels. As we explored this with our students, we realized that it was not only our leadership training that prepared students for successful leadership, but also our personal development and life curriculum.

Leadership skills, it turns out, were the skills of living a great life. For our students, leadership was not just a specific role in a certain organization, but a way of being. We realized that in addition to improving their own lives, everyone had a deep desire to be a positive influence on others, whether they had a designated role or not.

One thing we discovered over the years is fairly obvious, but incredibly powerful: human beings influence the behavior of other human beings. There is no casual interaction without influence. Students who are engaged in transforming their internal system (and hence their lives) often rise to positions of leadership in whatever area of life they are concerned with or in whatever setting they find themselves. This "accidental" by-product of transformational education is, for us, actually no accident. After all, transformational education and transformational leadership are two aspects of the same entity. As people learn, grow, and evolve, they become increasingly intentional about their influence in all situations and quite naturally discover themselves as leaders. As a result, we declared leadership explicitly as our mission and have codified the skills necessary to help students define the path of their leadership through six leadership levels and four leadership tracks.

A core assumption and perspective distinguishes our approach to leadership from all others with which we are familiar. We assume that leadership is both a hunger and a capacity inherent in all human beings, and that our leadership defines who we are and how the world perceives us. We assume that we are all leading all the time as we interact with others. Leadership is what we do to influence (or not influence) the world around us. While leadership is often discussed as the act or process of getting work done through others, we see it as the creative generation of experience in oneself and in others (Delves, Delves, Wright, & Wright, 2007). Where other leadership approaches discuss positions in organizations or treat leadership as a role and explore what leaders do, why they do it, how they do it, or how they came to do it, we approach leadership from an existential perspective. We see leadership as the continual process of leading ourselves and others to step into the unknown, to choose to be ever-evolving and everemerging, and to take responsibility for what we choose. Furthermore, we continue to fulfill Vygotsky's vision of ever-expanding individual development and to create an ever-expansive transformational process that impacts our students, our curriculum, and our organization.

As Wright students learn and grow and expand their sense of leadership and belonging at Wright, they simultaneously expand their engagement, sense of belonging, and mattering in the world. This process builds exponentially. Because as our students belong and matter more, they become more conscious of their positive influence on the world and are inspired to do more. Wright Performative Education at Wright guides and grounds these hungers, which all human beings share, with the belief that transformation of the world starts from the deepest yearning of the individual and from that deep longing is initiated a deep personal transformation that, through the power of our own choice, moves us from being to becoming, and from the life of more to the life of More.

As our students engage in their own continual transformation, evolution, and emergence, and so transform the leaders and curriculum, it is only to be expected that the Wright organization should (faithful to what we teach) be continually transforming and ever-evolving as well. What is exciting to us as we step into the future and as we choose our becoming, is that we do not know the Wright organization that is yet to be. We know what we have been, but as a learning organization committed to ongoing transformation, as creators of the tidal wave of our own transformation, we cannot yet know what we are to become.

CHAPTER FIVE

WRIGHT IN ACTION

*A Case Study of
Lifelong Learning*

CHAPTER FIVE

WRIGHT IN ACTION

A Case Study
of Lifelong Learning

INTRODUCTION

To illustrate how the developmental map described in this book guides a life quest for a great life, it is useful to look at an actual case study. This is a story of how Wright Performative Education takes the philosophical and psychological theories inherent in the Wright Model of Personal Growth and Development and helps you to change and transform.

This case history demonstrates how the Assignment Way of Living and an understanding of the Wright model allow you to have greater, more effective consciousness of yourself and your world. Consciousness allows you to be more effective in your interactions with the world, and it allows you to benefit more internally in the course of everyday living.

What follows is the story of one Wright student whose identity is masked. The story presents an overview of his growth story, reviews his journey through the levels of the Wright model, and shows how he worked assignments through each level.

CRAIG'S STORY

CRAIG ENTERED PERSONAL TRAINING and development work as a successful trumpet player in the Chicago area. He was not making the money he desired even though he was generally seen as successful. He was particularly vexed as to why he did not feel good about himself despite his success. His career had been meteoric, which he considered a fluke. His life was heavily influenced by scarcity. His relationships with women were unsatisfying, and he had difficulty developing lasting, fulfilling friendships with other men. He reported a fear of rejection; he manifested self-pity, or victimhood along with a lack of direction, and generally felt burdened by the work he needed to do to keep his career going.

He had been raised in a strict fundamentalist home with a domineering mother who allowed no honest, open communication. He concluded that the household in which he was raised operated on principles of deception and fear. His father was gay and eventually divorced his mother, despite their being leaders in their spiritual community.

Craig began by identifying his vision of the life he wanted. This was a revelation for him because he was more certain about what he would not be and do than he was about what he would do. His new vision included open, genuine, honest communication. It took a good deal of work for Craig to learn to operate from these principles of openness and expression of truth and joy. Operating in this new way required that he break many deeply ingrained rules and unconscious beliefs. In his learning lab, Craig worked on a series of assignments, one of which focused on expressing the truth in the moment. In doing this assignment, he was shocked to find that, instead of being rejected and criticized as he had been by his mother, many people welcomed his capacity to speak the truth.

He began relaxing with his music and taking more responsibility in his life. He experienced more fear because he took risks, but he did not suffer from it in the way he had in the past, because he now had a sense of direction. Craig began feeling more comfortable with women, too. Today he is a top musician nationally, succeeding at leading his own entertainment firm and earning more than he ever dreamed possible.

More important to Craig is his family life, one in which he and his wife are dynamically engaged in raising their two children. They embrace the learning and growing together and are thrilled by their progress as they learn and grow with their children. To show how Craig's journey was informed by the Wright Model of Personal Growth and Development and enhanced by the methodology and technology of Wright Performative Education, especially the Assignment Way of Living and coaching in the form of MORE Intimacy Training, the following sections provide a level-by-level view of Craig's growth and development. Included are the areas of life, principles, assignments, labs, and coaching, with some discussion of trainings and other growth activities.

CRAIG AT LEVEL ONE:
SCARCITY VS. TRUST WITH ALIVENESS RELATED TO BODY

Area – Body
Regressive Pole – Scarcity
Progressive Pole – Trust
Principle – Aliveness

Craig had always been aware that he was what he called, "tightly wound." He was not aware that his body was constantly under stress as he unconsciously fought to repress his natural urges. The primary area of life that relates to Level One is relationship to body. At the most primitive level and early ages, this relates to staying alive—the principle is aliveness. At more advanced ages, we may fear for our survival even when no imminent threat to our lives seems to be present. Fear is the primary emotion at this level. Craig was raised to fear displeasing others. As a result he repressed his aliveness, the primary principle operant at this level. He reported that he only felt fully alive and fearless in his music.

The progressive pole at this level of development is trust. You must overcome scarcity by being fully alive to develop this quality in your life. Trust relates to your confidence in the hospitality of the world. With trust, you express freely and protect where necessary. Craig uncovered unconscious beliefs in his MORE Intimacy Training (coaching) that the world was inhospitable and ready to reject him. This resulted in him tightening up and living his life in a muted way, except when he played music.

Trust is indicated and developed by your ability to express full aliveness, the positive principle, the polar opposite of deadness. The first order of business after creating a vision and setting goals for Craig was to help him learn to feel more alive in every way, including in his body and personal expression. Craig's challenge to be fully alive is a common one in the human condition if Nietzsche (1967) is to be believed. When you are born, you experience scarcity and you are vulnerable. You literally cannot live without the intervention of your parents. To the extent that they create a safe environment for you in the physical and emotional world, you learn to express your aliveness. You learn to trust the world. The world becomes your domain. In order to enhance Craig's expression, we needed to help him awaken his aliveness. Aliveness is suppressed originally by repressing impulses and emotions. Craig's initial lab assignments were designed to help him learn to identify and express his full range of emotions.

As Craig learned to trust his emotions, he was expressing more aliveness, risking more, and finding a good deal more enjoyment than he had imagined possible. He was more aware of all his emotions in the moment. He was shocked to discover how much fear ruled his life without his even noticing it. He was learning to live spontaneously, follow his urges, and experience a life of adventure.

CRAIG AT LEVEL TWO:
HUNGER VS. AFFIRMATION WITH PLAY RELATED TO SELF

Area – Self
Regressive Pole – Hunger
Progressive Pole – Affirmation
Principle – Play

Craig's awakening to his emotions allowed him to see the many ways he was actually abandoning himself internally. Relationship to self is the area of life that corresponds to Level Two, which is hunger and affirmation. As Craig began to pay more attention to himself, he noticed that he was confident but lacked self esteem. He knew he could do things well but did not feel inherently valuable or even good about himself. He was learning to affirm himself by noticing both the ways he felt good as well as the ways he felt bad.

Affirmation refers to your ability to see yourself objectively and accept yourself, thereby affirming your existence and accepting the truth of what and who you are. Affirmation results when your hunger needs are met. It means that you see yourself with positive regard. At Wright, we operate from a basic belief that you are okay. As Craig noticed more aspects of himself, he became increasingly aware of his hunger for affirmation. Hunger is your need for affirmation and it is also the state when you experience the lack of affirmation. It is the need to be seen. Hunger in your body is the sign that you need to be fed. Hunger in your psyche, likewise, indicates a need for nourishment. Craig had learned to notice himself in his early assignments and work with his MORE Intimacy trainer. Now in his learning laboratory, he was given assignments designed to provide him with more affirmation, like asking people what they liked about him. He progressed to one of the advanced assignments that develop affirmation skills, "group star," where he took center stage, faced his fear of rejection and ridicule, and did whatever came to his mind. He was developing new, livelier, more playful ways of being.

In these new ways of being, Craig was learning to identify, accept, and satisfy his hungers. He was taking responsibility for these yearnings and expressing them, especially in times when he needed affirmation from the outside because he was not capable of giving it to himself. This way he was learning, growing, and being nourished.

Assignments to play, make mistakes, and be "little" were paired with questions in Craig's MORE Intimacy Training. He was learning to relax and be himself in ways he never imagined. His interactions with the world were becoming more fulfilling. Whether pleasurable or painful, he was learning. Play is the principle that operates at this level. By expressing his hunger in play, he automatically interacted with others and opened himself up to receive the nourishment that he craved. Experiencing this affirmation, he found that he was learning and growing at remarkable rates. He was shocked to discover that hunger is a natural human function, just as physical hunger is natural, and never over.

For example, as a teacher of music, Craig found that interacting fully with his classes was nourishing for him and his pupils. He reported significant fulfillment and a new drive to watch them succeed. He loved giving recognition for a job well done, and was surprised at the warmth and nourishment that came from empathizing with the struggles of his students.

Craig was pleased to find an increasing belief in his worth and this manifested in his expanding ability to serve and meet the needs of those whom he touched. He was surprised to discover that his ability to touch others was directly proportional to his ability to have his own needs met. He felt proud to see his ability to take responsibility for his own nourishment and touch others. To the extent that he expressed his hunger with full play, he was affirmed, whether the responses of others were positive or not. He had internalized a great deal of affirmation and was able to carry it more and more with him. He was often even able to affirm himself in the absence of direct affirmation from the world around him. This allowed him to move increasingly into difficult areas in his life, to go for long periods of time without direct affirmation, to reach for his highest vision, and to engage in a worthwhile quest. His expanding sense of fulfillment led, in his mind, to meeting and connecting with his future wife, to whom he is now married, the development of his family, and his sense of life mission, serving society fully, so that he can live, as he put it, in a more loving, supportive, just, equitable, and truthful world.

CRAIG AT LEVEL THREE:
REACTIVITY VS. ASSERTION WITH INTENTION RELATED TO FAMILY AND INTIMACY

Area – Family and Intimacy
Regressive Pole – Reactivity
Progressive Pole – Assertion
Principle – Intention

Craig completed a lab assignment to inventory all of the thoughts and feelings he had not delivered to his family of origin. Family of origin and creation is the area of life that coincides with Level Three. Craig was amazed to see how many undelivered communications he had accumulated and he found the inventory unsettling when he thought about delivering them. The cost to him was high. He realized that all of his relationships were similarly marked by withholding and this seemed to him to relate directly to some level of dissatisfaction in most of his life. He was passive in ways that embarrassed him. Assertion was difficult and he now saw why some of his friends and bosses had labeled him passive-aggressive.

Assertion is the progressive pole of this level and intention is the principle. Reactivity is the regressive pole. This is marked developmentally by what is often called the "terrible twos," a time when the child asserts his will by resisting. Craig was acutely aware that he had never really been assertive and set a goal to become more assertive. In his MORE Intimacy Training, Craig and his coach focused on his delivering judgments and criticisms. He was shocked to discover the degree to which he was dishonest with everyone. Expressing his judgments to his trainer was a revelation. His critical perceptions did not drive his trainer away. He was still a long way, however, from being able to do the assertiveness assignments in his lab.

Craig did lab assignments to ask for things and disagree with others, and he eventually built his way up to delivering criticisms to group members. He was learning to assert his will with conscious intent. The principle "intention" is play with direction and desire, just as "play" was aliveness in interaction. It is the principle whereby we create the world around us, with assertion as the final result. Assertion is the expression of positive desire. As Craig began to acknowledge his desires, he was shocked to see how many desires and agendas he had that had previously gone unexpressed. He realized that he had been largely reactive, rather than expressive in his life. Reactivity is the regressive aspect of assertion.

Craig saw how he expressed his displeasure by quietly not complying with others' desires, rather than openly asserting his contrary desires and will. He used assignments in the assertiveness series to open the power locked in his passive aggressive silences. The lab assignment to openly say "No" to others was another revelation. He felt stronger and most of the time people did not reject him. He was learning to harness conscious, positive intent. Intentionality is the principle operating behind saying "No," "Yes," or "Give it to me." The "No" is reactivity. The "Yes" is assertion. Without being able to say, "No," it is impossible to say, "Yes."

Craig realized how his open expression of intent was repressed as a child when he began interacting with the world, wanting to grab, wanting to push away. His mother would not tolerate his assertiveness so he withdrew when others were expressing their will in the terrible twos. He had never really learned to say an open, honest "No." His hunger and dependence had kept him more compliant. Craig realized that open, honest assertion would likely be a lifelong challenge for him, a challenge he felt up to with the foundation he developed in lab.

In one particularly illuminating, challenging lab assignment, Craig was invited to express his intention fully, and group members were instructed to stand up. They were told to keep standing until he expressed full intention to have them sit down. His job was to get all of them to sit down. At first Craig struggled, but he later reported that it was as if something had snapped inside of him and he felt as if he tapped all the power of rage and absolute intent and lab members sat down quickly.

Craig learned that tapping the power of his intent opened new possibilities in all that he did. His band was recording and receiving rave reviews. They were even voted one of the best national bands in their category by the prestige publication in his field. Craig knew that he could not always win, but he learned to relish trying. He felt an affinity to the stories of the home run king, Babe Ruth, who was also a leader in strike-outs. Craig was living his life more fully, swinging with gusto, but not expecting every swing to lead to a home run. He felt that his life was an extension of his desires, his own creation for the first time. He was no longer a victim going along but an artist painting his own tableau.

CRAIG AT LEVEL FOUR:
CONFORMITY VS. EXPRESSION WITH TRUTH RELATED TO FRIENDS AND OTHERS

Area – Friends and Others
Regressive Pole – Conformity
Progressive Pole – Expression
Principle – Truth

Craig had always thought of himself as an individualist. He prided himself on his choice in music and friends. As a result, he was particularly disturbed when he began to realize how much of his life was governed by the desire to avoid rejection and fit in, rather than truly expressing himself. Friends and others is the area of life at Level Four, and conformity is the regressive pole.

Conformity is grounded in the desire to belong. It is a necessary life skill; however, as you saw above, most of the population overuses this skill, thereby avoiding rejection and conforming to the exclusion of full, genuine personal expression. Craig was no exception. Being overweight most of his life, he was especially sensitive to being called "fatty" or some other insult. He realized he had never really expressed his will fully in any group, let alone expressed the truth of his experience to his highest vision, the principle of this level, which is also simply referred to as truth. He had complained and criticized in private, but never had stood for his beliefs, even in opposition to the group in which he belonged. Truth is the principle of intentionality in relationship. It is play and aliveness in the purest form. It is the expression of the self in relationship to others.

According to G. M. Durst (1982), 80% of the general population fails, as a rule, to express the truth of their experience to their highest vision in day-to-day life. Craig was no exception. He saw how fear of rejection had caused him to shut down, to hold back expressing his truth, and to let bullies dominate too many situations. This had left him mired in the same self-loathing that he realized had also defined his father's life.

Craig's big breakthrough at this level came with the assignments that required him to deliver judgments and interact more freely with lab members. He was shocked, once again, to hear that his real thoughts did not cause people to shun him or crumble. To the contrary, lab members began trusting him more and found him to be a more contributory member. As he began expressing his feelings, he left his band rehearsals feeling afraid that the members would reject him, but they did not. They did not always agree, but it was more his fear than the reality of their rejection that caused him to be afraid.

Expressing the truth of your experiences is a very complex skill, one that Craig and his wife are still learning and teaching their children. Craig and his wife are acutely aware of the desire to belong to each other and the family, and to submit one's will to the group where appropriate, but they are committed to realizing their individual satisfaction and standards. They seek to help each member of the family learn to express the truth of their experience to their highest vision, so that each can be a creative force in whatever group they belong.

They feel that telling the truth frees them, even though it is often difficult and late in coming. They do it because they know that telling the truth may sometimes be painful, enraging, or joyful, but it almost always leads to more aliveness and clarity in relationships. It helps them learn to accept themselves. They strive for a security in belonging, withstanding a certain amount of disapproval, and still being able to feel okay. Craig and his wife know that expressing the truth of their experience is a very complex skill, and requires practice. They are doing their best to integrate this into their house with family meetings and intentional periods of what they call "getting current" with each other.

CRAIG AT LEVEL FIVE:
STRIVING VS. PURPOSE WITH COMMITMENT RELATED TO WORK AND PLAY

Area – Work and Play
Regressive Pole – Striving
Progressive Pole – Purpose
Principle – Commitment

Commitment, the primary principle operating at Level Five, is expression of truth in dedication of your life—the dedication of your fully developed self towards some ideal, goal, or object. The regressive pole, striving, is commitment toward goals for regressive reasons, such as scarcity, hunger, reactivity, or conformity.

This is a normal phase of development where Craig realized he had become stuck. Highly talented at the trumpet, he had dedicated himself as a musician, but not as a human being. He realized that his earlier shortcomings in his career were not because of his music but because he had not committed himself as a full person. He had wanted to win the career game so that he could prove that he was okay, instead of directly meeting his hunger needs. He wanted to earn more money and record a hit album so that he could prove his value and overcome his scarcity.

Craig was stuck at striving because he had not directly recognized the scarcity, hunger, reactivity, and conformity needs that arose when he left college. In his growth work, as he learned to meet these needs, his commitment deepened, and he was able to really strive and commit. Striving fully expressed ultimately leads to a sense of purpose and meaning in your life. And this was so with Craig. Craig was becoming a peer with his MORE Intimacy Training coach, and he was doing an excellent job with his final seniority assignments in his learning lab. He was an effective facilitator, and his life purpose assignment was an inspiration to lab members. He applied this in his daily life, and his deep sense of purpose in his family, his profession, and his community is an inspiration to many who know him. Craig was ready to complete his lab and MORE Intimacy Training and continue the adventure of developing in consciousness throughout the remainder of his life.

Craig learned that he was increasingly able to align with life itself. He was facing challenges he had previously avoided and he was developing an expanding ability to be a blessing to the environments in which he found himself. He does not necessarily look at it this way on a daily basis, but he thinks this is true because he feels so blessed. Craig knows that striving frequently overlays his emerging reactivity, hunger, and scarcity, so he is vigilant. He knows that he is likely to stop at "bigger-is-better" to cover his real hunger needs to belong. He knows to watch for his denial of the regressive needs and to meet them. He knows that external success alone does not provide a sense of fulfillment and affirmation. Despite his financial success, he knows that it alone will not satisfy deep-seated feelings of scarcity. He has been feeling his striving changing to an even stronger sense of purpose and meaning emerging in his life. He has been feeling a more balanced perspective on life issues, with his striving changing to a strong sense of mission. In his new way of being, he supports family, employees, clients, and others in applying themselves fully to their ideals with a sense of purpose too.

CRAIG AT LEVEL SIX:
SUPERIORITY VS. AUTHORITY WITH RESPONSIBILITY RELATED TO PRINCIPLES AND SOCIETY

Area – Principles and Society
Regressive Pole – Superiority
Progressive Pole – Authority
Principle – Responsibility

Much of Craig's personal development since his graduation from his Wright learning lab is at Level Six, where he is learning to live with full responsibility. Responsibility is the principle whereby you create your reality. Its regressive aspect is superiority. Having lived with purpose, Craig realizes that he has learned a great deal, and he can use this to serve others, or to manipulate, to manage, and to stay above others when he really yearns to belong, be known, and be accepted. It is responsibility that helps you move from superiority to authority. In his marriage, Craig finds this particularly challenging. He often tends to act superior to his wife. Rather than taking responsibility for his hunger needs directly, he "helps" her. With responsibility, however, he claims the gaps in his behavior rather than blaming her. As he ceases blaming her or excusing himself, he becomes increasingly the author of his own existence. In authority there is no longer anyone to blame. Living with authority, he is narrowing the gap between his behavior and his stated ideals, thereby moving closer and closer to living with full consciousness in connection to the source of all life as fully as possible.

CRAIG AT LEVEL SEVEN:
CONSCIOUSNESS RELATED TO LIFE PURPOSE AND SPIRITUALITY

Area – Life Purpose and Spirituality
Non-dualistic Consciousness
Principle – Transcendental principles such as love,
compassion, forgiveness, acceptance, grace

In consciousness you are your commitment. Craig will continue to seek to live by the non-dualistic transcendental principles of love, compassion, forgiveness, grace, and acceptance for the remainder of his life.

CONCLUSION

Craig exemplifies the three major theories Wright employs in providing a developmental map of life to help the lifelong learner analyze, strategize, and track personal growth and development using the Wright Model of Personal Growth and Development and Wright Performative Education. The synergy of the three seems to lead to a result that is truly greater than the mere sum of the parts. The model is eminently practical while allowing the student to learn from and plumb the depths of some of the greatest thinkers of our or any time: luminaries from Freud to Nietzsche, Adler to Heidegger, and Sartre to Maslow.

At the same time, Craig's story is just an introduction to the dynamic interplay among the three models that makes it particularly useful to you. It is important to understand that we are constantly switching among the levels depending on the unfinished business we bring to any situation. This unfinished business causes us to operate at the regressive pole of earlier developmental levels depending on our makeup. To accurately reflect Wright's holistic view of consciousness, each level of the developmental model should be viewed as the growth ring in the trunk of a tree—all rings being present at any cross-section of the tree. All are present in some form from birth just as the acorn contains the full potential for an oak. You may focus on the dynamics of a specific level at a particular time in lifelong development training but all levels are available at all times, and you are capable of shifting from one level to another with a change in circumstances, moment to moment.

So you begin to see that even though developmental theory would make it seem that you move on to one level and leave behind the prior level, this is only an illusion. You are constantly being stimulated by your world and it is as if buttons get pressed causing reactions in you. These reactions are generally defined by our internal development related to the area and issue. One issue and situation may evoke Level Two Hunger in you, and you will need to hearken to the principle of play to meet a hunger need and be affirmed. Another situation may evoke Level Three Reactivity, and you will best focus on intent to meet your reactivity need and move to a position of assertion.

Accordingly, the Wright model allows you to identify the level at which you operate in any given situation, just as it did for Craig throughout his journey. You can also identify the area of life and the principles you need to enhance in order to progress. Identification of the regressive form of a level brings you insight about what you need to improve and how you can succeed in doing so. The identification of the level also gives you an idea of the principle that you need to learn to use to meet your regressive need. In this way, the model acts as a guide to help you deal with issues you face in the present.

Craig's story also shows how the Wright model provides a framework for understanding prior choices. It helps you reconsider these choices in order to understand yourself and strategize future actions. By doing this, you are beginning to strategize your development and genuinely live at higher levels of consciousness. The higher levels of consciousness: Level Five Commitment, Level Six Authority, and Level Seven Spirituality are limited if the earlier level regressive issues are not worked through to completion. You can access those levels but you do not have anything approaching mastery without a sufficient foundation in the earlier levels: Level One Aliveness, Level Two Play, Level Three Intent, and Level Four Truth. The Wright model gives you a powerful tool for daily success as well as a framework to strategize and within which you can monitor your growth. It enables you to learn from and rework earlier life choices.

Nobody has developed fully and completely. As you develop throughout your life, you face new situations that cause you to need to manage your regressive needs of scarcity, hunger, reactivity, and conformity. The Wright Model of Personal Growth and Development provides a dynamic framework to understand these situations and your reactions and to identify the need you are experiencing. Wright Performative Education gives you a learning environment to meet unmet needs, complete unfinished business, and experiment with the new behaviors you need to learn in order to develop to your full potential, to transform to more fulfilling levels of consciousness, and to engage in life as an unfolding adventure of becoming.

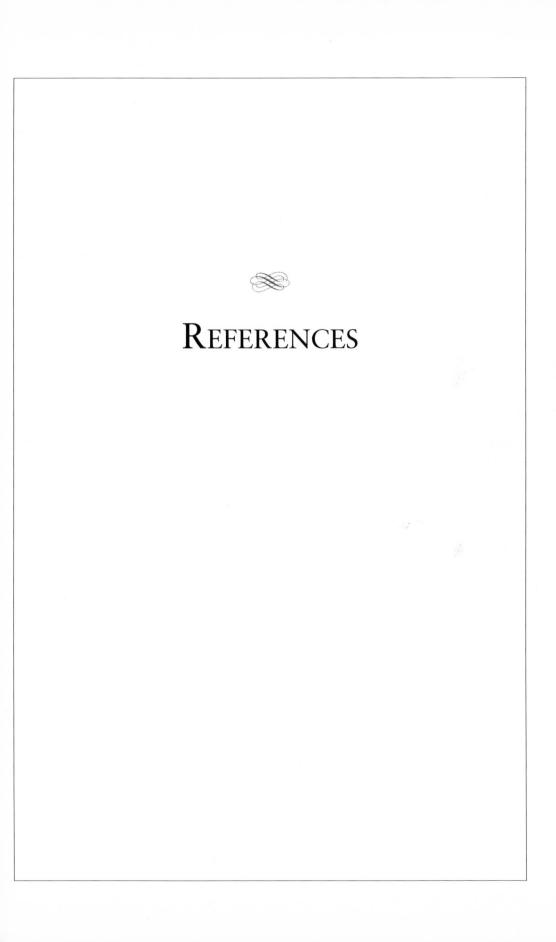

REFERENCES

REFERENCES

Adler, A. (1962). *Understanding human nature.* (W.B. Wolfe, Trans.). London: Allen and Unwin. (Original work published 1927).

Adler, A., & Brett, C. (1997). *Understanding life: An Introduction to the Psychology of Alfred Adler.* Oxford: Oneworld.

Aristotle, & Ostwald, M. (1962). *Nicomachean ethics.* Library of liberal arts, 75. Indianapolis [Ind.]: Bobbs-Merrill.

BBC News. (2005). *Infomania worse than marijuana.* Retrieved March 23, 2008, from http://news.bbc.co.uk/2/hi/uk_news/4471607.stm.

Beames, T. B. (1984). *A student's glossary of Adlerian terminology.* Chicago, IL: Adler Institute of Chicago.

Berne, E. (1961). *Transactional analysis in psychotherapy.* New York: Grove Press.

Bowen, M. (1985). *Family systems in the clinical practice.* Lanham, MD: Lanham: Rowman and Littlefield.

Boyd, R. D., & Myers, J. G. (1988). Transformative education. *International Journal of Lifelong Education, 7* (4), Oct-Dec pp. 261-284.

Bruner, J. (1971). *The relevance of education.* New York: Norton.

Bugental, J. F. T. (1967). *Challenges of humanistic psychology.* New York: McGraw-Hill.

Burns, J. (1978). *Leadership.* New York: Harper and Row.

Cohen, J. (2004, May 19). Lloyd Banks Feeds The 'Hunger.' *Billboard.* Retrieved October 22, 2007, from http://www.billboard.com/bbcom/search/google/article_display.jsp?vnu_content_id=1000514401#

Collins, J. (2001). *Good to great: why some companies make the leap…and others don't.* New York: Collins Business.

Dewey, J. (1938). *Experience and education.* The Kappa Delta Pi lecture series, [no. 10]. New York: Macmillan.

Driscoll, M. P. (1994). *Psychology of learning for instruction.* Boston: Allyn and Bacon.

Durst, G.M. (1982). *Management by responsibility.* Evanston, IL: Training Systems, Inc.

English, Oliver and Finch, Stuart. (1964). *Introduction to psychiatry.* New York: W. W. Norton & Company

Erikson, Erik (1950, reissue 1993). *Childhood and Society.* New York: W. W. Norton & Company

Evans, C. (1982). *Moral Stage Development and Knowledge of Kohlberg's Theory.* Journal of Experimental Education, Vol. 51, pp. 14-17.

Firestone, R.(1987). The "voice": The dual nature of guilt reactions. *The American Journal of Psychoanalysis.* 47(3), Fall pp. 210-229.

Freud, S., Strachey, J., Freud, A, Rothgeb, C.L. & Richards, A. (1953). *The standard edition of the complete psychological works of Sigmund Freud.* London: Hogarth Press.

Fromm, E. (1981). *To have or to be.* New York: Bantam Books.

Fuller, R. B. (1981). *Critical path.* New York: St. Martin's Press.

Graves, C.W. (2002). *Introduction to the psychological map.* Santa Barbara, CA: ECLET Publishing.

Graves, C.W. (2002). *Levels of human existence.* Santa Barbara, CA: ECLET Publishing.

Harvey, P. (1990). *An introduction to Buddhism: Teachings, history and practices.* Cambridge [England]: Cambridge University Press.

Heidegger, M. (1962). *Being and time.* New York: Harper.

Holzman, L. (2000). *Performative psychology: An untapped resource for educators.* Manuscript submitted for publication, East Side Institute for Short Term Psychology.

Holzman, L. (2006). *Lev Vygotsky and the new performative psychology: Implications for business and organizations.* The Social Construction of Organizations: CBS Press.

James, W. (1890). *The principles of psychology.* New York: H. Holt and company.

Jung, C. G. (1939). *Modern man in search of a soul.* New York: Harcourt, Brace.

Kierkegaard, S. (1938). *Purity of heart is to will one thing.* New York: Harper.

Kierkegaard, S. (1959). *Either/or Vol. 2* (D.F. Swenson & L.M. Swanson, Trans.). Garden City, NY: Doubleday. (Original work published 1843).

Kierkegaard, S. (1973). *Fear and trembling and sickness until death.* (W. Lowrie, Trans.). Princeton, MA: Princeton University Press. (Original work published 1843).

Kierkegaard, S. (1980). *The concept of anxiety: A simple psychologically orienting deliberation on the dogmatic issue of hereditary sin.* Princeton: Princeton University Press.

Kierkegaard, S. (1992) *Either/or: A fragment of life* (V. Eremita, Trans.). New York: Penguin Classics. (Original work published 1843)

Kierkegaard, S., Hong, H.V., & Hong, E.H. (1962). *Works of love: some Christian reflections in the form of discourses.* New York: Harper.

Kohlberg, L. (1984). *The psychology of moral development: the nature and validity of moral stages.* San Francisco: Harper Row.

Lee, W. (1999). *A comparison of the spiral dynamics map with other maps,* [Electronic Version]. Retrieved March 3, 2005, from http://www.clarewgraves.com/research_content/CG&others/intro.html

Lindeman, E. (1926). *The meaning of adult education.* New York: New Republic.

Loevinger, Jane (1970). *Measuring Ego Development: Construction and Use of a Sentence Completion Test Proquest Info & Learning,* Jossey-Bass Behavioral Science Series)

Maddi, S., & Kobasa, S. (1984). *The hardy executive: health under stress.* Homewood, IL: Dow Jones Irwin.

Maslow, A.H. (1968). *Toward a psychology of being,* (2nd ed.). New York: Van Nostrand Reinhold.

May, R. (1967). Psychology and the human dilemma. In May, R., Angel, E. & Ellenberger, H. (Eds.), *Existence; a new dimension in psychiatry and psychology* (2nd ed.)(p. 50). New York: Basic Books.

May, R. (1996). *The meaning of anxiety.* New York: W.W. Norton Company.

May, R. (1998). *Power and innocence: A search for the source of violence.* New York: Norton, W. W. & Company, Inc.

Medlock, G. (1986). *Sartre's theory of existential psychoanalysis and its implications for existential psychotherapy.* Unpublished doctoral dissertation, University of Ann Arbor, MI.

Merriam, S.B., & Caffarella, R.S. (1991). *Learning in adulthood: a comprehensive guide.* The Jossey-Bass higher end adult education series. San Francisco: Jossey-Bass.

Mezirow, J. (1991). *Transformative dimensions of adult learning.* San Francisco: Jossey-Bass.

Mezirow, J. (2000). *Learning as transformation: Critical perspectives on a theory in progress.* New York: Jossey-Bass.

Mialaret, G. (1976). *The contribution of fundamental sciences to educational sciences.* The International Moral Education Congress. Paris: Editions de l'Epi (EPI).

Miller, J.P. & Seller, W. (1990) *Curriculum: perspectives and practice.* Toronto: Copp Clark Pitman.

Moore, R. (2002). *Transforming fire: Understanding, accessing, and regulating psychic and spiritual energy* [Audio recording]. Audio # RM41. Chicago: C.G. Jung Institute

Morningstar, J. (1981) *Spiritual psychology: A new age course for body, mind and spirit.* Milwaukee: Transformations

Nietzsche, F. (1967). *On the genealogy of morals and ecce homo* (W. Kaufmann, Trans.). New York: Vintage. (Original works published 1887-1889)

Nietzsche, F. W., Nietzsche, F. W. & Kaufmann, W. A. (1967). *On the genealogy of morals.* New York: Vintage Books.

O'Sullivan, E., & Morrell, A. (2002) *Expanding the boundaries of transformative learning: essays on theory and praxis.* New York: Palgrave Press.

Plato, & Jowett, B. (1941). *Plato's The Republic.* New York: The Modern library. (Original work published 360BC).

Plato. (2003). *The Last Days of Socrates* (H. Tredennick, Trans., & H. Tarrant, Ed.) New York: Penguin Classics. (Original work published 360 BC)

Quinn, R. E. (1996). *Deep change: Discovering the leader within.* San Francisco, Jossey-Bass.

Rath, T. & Clifton, D. (2004) *How full is your bucket? Positive strategies for work and life.* Gallup Press, New York.

Rogers, C. (1961). *On becoming a person: A therapist's view of psychotherapy.* London: Constable.

Sameroff, A., & Chandler, M. (1975). Reproductive risk and the continuum of caretaking causality. In F. Horowitz (Ed). *Review of child development* (pp. 187-244). Chicago: University of Chicago Press.

Sartre, J. P. (1956). *Being and nothingness: An essay on phenomenological ontology.* New York: Baker and Taylor.

Sartre, J. P. (1978). *Being and nothingness* (H. Barnes, Trans.). New York: Quoka. (Original work published 1943)

Sartre, J. P. (1993). *Essays in existentialism.* New York: Citadel Press.

Schulman, B. H., & Dreikurs, S. G. (1978). *The contributions of Rudolph Dreikurs to the theory and practice of Individual Psychology.* Journal of Individual Psychology, 34, 163.

Seligman, M. E. P. (2002). *Authentic happiness: Using the new positive psychology to realize your potential for lasting fulfillment.* New York: Free Press.

Senge, P. M. (1990). *The fifth discipline: the art and practice of the learning organization.* New York: Doubleday/Currency.

Sheehy, G. (1976). *Passages. Predictable crises of adult life.* New York: E. P. Dutton/Bantam.

The Compact Oxford English Dictionary. (1991). Oxford, England: Clarendon Press.

Tillich, P. (1952). *The courage to be.* New Haven: Yale University Press.

Von Bertalanffy, L. 1968. *General system theory: Foundations, development, applications.* New York: George Braziller.

Vygotsky, L. (1978). *Mind in society: The development of higher psychological processes.* Massachusetts: Harvard University Press.

Watts, A. (1960). *The spirit of Zen: a way of life, work and art in the Far East.* New York: Grove Press.

Watts, A. (1971). *Behold the spirit; a study in the necessity of mystical religion.* New York: Pantheon Books.

Whitehead, B. D. & Popenoe, D. (2006). *The state of our unions: The social health of marriage in America.* Retrieved October 21, 2008, from http://marriage.rutgers.edu/Publications/SOOU/TEXTSOOU2006.htm#Divorce_Endnotes

Wilber, Ken (1980). *The Atman project, a transpersonal view of human development.* Wheaton: Quest Books.

Wink, J., & Putney, L. (2002). *A Vision of Vygotsky.* Boston: Allyn & Bacon.

Wolfert, R. (1997). *Self in experience, gestalt therapy, science and Buddhism: an evolving synthesis.* Presented at the New York Institute for Gestalt Therapy.

Woolf, Vernon. (1990). *Holodynamics: How to develop and manage your personal power.* Tucson AZ: Harbinger House.

Wright, J. (2003). *There must be more than this: Finding more life, love, and meaning by overcoming your soft addictions.* New York: Broadway Books.

Wright, J. (2005). *The one decision.* New York: Tarcher/Penguin.

Wright, J. (2006). *The soft addiction solution.* New York: Tarcher/Penguin.

Wright, J. S. (1982). An integrative model of parent involvement. In M. Peters (Ed.), *Building an alliance for children: Parents and professionals.* Seattle: University of Washington PDAS.

Wright, J. S., Granger, R., & Sameroff, A. (1984). Parental acceptance and developmental handicap. In J. Blancher (Ed.), *Severely handicapped young children and their families: Research in review* (pp. 51-90). Orlando, FL: Academic Press.

Wright, J., Wright, R., Delves, D. & Delves, D. (2008). *Fielding ELC 752 leadership and change.* Unpublished manuscript, Fielding Graduate University, Santa Barbara, CA.

Wright, R. (2008). Comprehensive Essay. Unpublished manuscript, Fielding Graduate University, Santa Barbara, CA.

Wright, R. J., & Medlock, G. (1994). *Facing our bad faith: The challenge of personal and spiritual growth.* Unpublished manuscript, Presented at the 13th Human Science Research Conference, West Hartford, CT.

Wright, R., & Medlock, G. (1992). *Applied comprehensive developmental psychology, an existential-developmental paradigm.* First Conference on Existential Psychotherapy, Mexico.

Wright, R., Medlock, G., & Peterson, J. (1994). *On the importance of integrative theory in psychotherapy: An existential-developmental perspective.* The Conference on Integrative and Eclectic Psychotherapy, Lyon, France.

Yalom, I. (1980). *Existential psychotherapy.* New York: Basic Books Inc.

Yeaxlee, B. A. (1929). *Lifelong Education.* London: Cassell.

Zebroski, J. (1994). *Thinking through theory: Vygotskian perspectives on the teaching of writing.* New Hampshire: Boynton Cook.

Zimmerman, M.E. (1981). *Eclipse of the self: The development of Heidegger's concept of authenticity.* Athens, OH: Ohio University Press. About the Authors

About the Authors

For over 35 years, Drs. Judith and Robert Wright have trained and coached thousands of individuals, some over the course of decades through a myriad of challenges and opportunities from health to finances to family and relationships to career, some from the point of graduating from business school to being top executives in multi-national public corporations. Initially working in their own individual practices, they joined forces to cofound Wright in Chicago in 1997.

In addition, the Wrights cofounded the Wright Graduate Institute, offering masters and doctoral degrees in Transformational Learning, Leadership, and Coaching. Drs. Wright have become two of the country's foremost experts on transformational leadership, having established the Foundation for Transformational Leadership as well as The Transformational Leadership Symposium, which convened leadership experts from around the nation to recognize cutting-edge leaders including Brad Anderson, former CEO of Best Buy, as well as the 2012 Award recipient, Dr. Muhammad Yunus.

Dr. Robert Wright

Considered by many to be one of the leading thinkers in human development, Dr. Robert Wright (www.drbobwright.com) is an internationally recognized visionary, educator, program developer, author, speaker, entrepreneur, consultant, and executive coach. Recognized as a top executive coach by *Crain's Chicago Business*, he has coached CEOs across the country from leading-name public companies to entrepreneurial startups. Dr. Wright's revolutionary Wright Model of Personal Growth and Development provides a much-needed practical application of theory into everyday life, helping hundreds of thousands to understand themselves, strategize, and take action to reach their potential. Called "the most powerful comprehensive model of its kind," this model forms the core curriculum at Wright.

Dr. Robert Wright's revolutionary personal and professional training and development methodology leads not only to significant professional success, but also to fulfillment in all life areas. Dr. Robert Wright has demonstrated success in a wide variety of areas. He is an outstanding radio and television personality, delivering what author Andrew Harvey calls his "hard light." His books on purpose in business and people skills have been translated into multiple languages and sold over 200,000 copies around the globe. And his nationally-acclaimed employee assistance and managed mental health firm, Human Effectiveness, Inc., was rated top in the nation by Mercer Meidinger Medical Audit as well as Arthur Andersen.

Dr. Robert Wright established Living Visions, a personal growth business; founded the Men's Guild, a powerful men's organization for a new model of manhood; and established Be Heard, an organization to promote environmentally conscious political action. His education, coaching, and leadership research led to the development of what he named Grounded Leadership, an invaluable facilitative part of the transformational leader's tool box.

Dr. Robert Wright's deep belief in human potential has guided his mission to bring cutting-edge and traditional human emergence technologies into practical everyday use for the conscious evolution of humanity—most recently founding Wright, an organization focused on personal transformation and leadership development, the Wright Graduate Institute and the Foundation for Transformational Leadership. Dr. Robert Wright has completed a BA in Sociology, MA in Communications, MSW in Clinical Social Work, and a Doctorate in Education, Leadership, and Change.

DR. JUDITH WRIGHT

A media favorite, sought-after speaker, respected leader, best-selling author, world-class coach, and corporate consultant, Dr. Judith Wright (www.judithwright.com) wrote *There Must Be More Than This* (Random House/Broadway Books), *The One Decision*, and *The Soft Addiction Solution* (Penguin/Tarcher) to share her proven personal transformation methodologies with a broader audience. A pioneer in the field of human development, Dr. Judith Wright first rose to national prominence by developing innovative education and early childhood development programs for those with developmental disabilities. These experiences fueled her passion for developing human potential and strengthened her deep-rooted commitment to help people live great lives.

Dr. Judith Wright then applied the profound insights she discovered to the general population, spurring people from all walks of life to significant success in personal transformation, leadership development, and personal goal fulfillment. In addition to her pioneering work as the president and co-founder of Wright, an organization focused on personal transformation and leadership development and the Wright Graduate Institute, she is the founder of SOFIA (Society of Femininity in Action), providing revolutionary leadership training for women.

She is a sought-after expert who has appeared as a featured lifestyle expert and coach on ABC's *20/20*, *Oprah*, *Good Morning America*, the *Today* show and hundreds of radio and television shows. Called the "world's ultimate expert," her work has appeared in over 80 magazines and newspapers around the globe including *Marie Claire, Fitness Magazine, Health, Better Homes and Gardens, Shape, The New York Daily News, The Chicago Tribune, The Boston Herald,* and *The San Francisco Chronicle.* Dr. Wright completed a comprehensive ten-year research initiative exploring the process of and components for living a great life. This research forms the basis for the pioneering Evolating Process, which has changed the lives of thousands of people. Dr. Wright has her BA in psychology, her MA in education and counseling and her doctorate in Educational Leadership and Change.